The Spirit Unfettered

Edmund J. Rybarczyk

a PARACLETE GUIDE

D1226040

PARACLETE PRESS
BREWSTER, MASSACHUSETTS

The Spirit Unfettered: Protestant Views on the Holy Spirit

2010   First Printing

Copyright © 2010 by Edmund J. Rybarczyk

ISBN: 978-1-55725-654-6

Library of Congress Cataloging-in-Publication Data
Rybarczyk, Edmund J. (Edmund John), 1961-
  The Spirit unfettered : Protestant views on the Holy Spirit /
Edmund J. Rybarczyk.
     p. cm.
  Includes bibliographical references (p.   ).
  ISBN 978-1-55725-654-6
  1. Holy Spirit—History of doctrines. 2. Theologians—History. 3.
Protestant churches—Doctrines—History. I. Title.
  BT119.R93 2010
  231'.3—dc22   2010031830

10 9 8 7 6 5 4 3 2 1

Published by Paraclete Press
Brewster, Massachusetts
www.paracletepress.com
Printed in the United States of America

Contents

Introduction

*W*HY STUDY THE HOLY SPIRIT? To that question there are many good answers. Christians will want to know what is true about the beliefs their faith espouses. I have long said to my students, "You are banking your identity, let alone your eternal destiny, on this faith. So you owe it to yourself to know what it teaches."

As the Bible reveals it, the Holy Spirit is God's means of activity in daily life. The Holy Spirit is how (or better *who*) God accomplishes things in history. Jesus of Nazareth himself experienced an intimate relationship with both God his Father and the Holy Spirit. In the Gospels of Matthew, Mark, and Luke Jesus openly asserted that he was variously preaching the gospel, performing miraculous signs, and driving out demons by the power of the Spirit, who empowered him to glorify God the Father. After his resurrection Jesus sent his Spirit to do the same things for, in, and through the church that the Spirit had done for, in, and through Jesus: preach the gospel, perform miracles, and drive out unclean spirits. And, as the New Testament clarifies, the apostolic church glorified God the Father just as Jesus did. In learning about the Holy Spirit contemporary Christians will recall God's powerful involvement in biblical history.

Even more, the New Testament passages about Jesus' experience of God's Spirit, together with those passages about

Jesus' relationship with his heavenly Father, were profoundly suggestive to the postapostolic ancient church about God's own identity. Why does the Church teach the doctrine of the Trinity? More than anything else, it is because the biblical witness shows that Jesus related in a unique way to both God the Father and God the Spirit. In this book, we will focus more on the work and effects of the Spirit on believers and creation than on Trinitarian formulations, but twentieth-century theologians in particular, because of renewed interest in God's Spirit, have reexamined the doctrine of the Trinity. We will touch on some of those fresh formulations in our later chapters.

This book offers a survey of what various Protestant theologians have asserted about the Holy Spirit. Through them we will learn about the God we serve. But not only theologians know God or know about God! Millions of believers through history knew the living God. Evagrius Ponticus (AD 345–99) once said, "The true theologian is the one who prays." Anyone who seeks God is to some extent a theologian. But the reason we consult the opinion of trained theologians concerns the matter of wisdom. We learn from those who have spent their lives studying the Scriptures, reflecting on God's existence, worshiping him, and extending all of that toward life. In looking to their wisdom we avoid reinventing the wheel.

Still further, why study *Protestant* theologians concerning God's Spirit? In answering that we begin to move toward some of the *in-house* nuances that make the Christian traditions and tributaries distinct from one another. To be sure, all Christians believe that God is triune, that God mysteriously exists as the persons of (or more technically, distinctions of) Father, Son, and Spirit. Let me clarify. In teaching about God, ancient church faith-confessions and creeds used the Greek philosophical term *hypostasis* (distinction or person) and its plural form *hypostases* together with *ousia* (essence). Using those terms in precise ways precluded the idea that God was three independent persons, which results in tritheism (three Gods); those technical terms also enabled the church to maintain the unique identities of the Father, the Son, and the Spirit. The classic formula, used by Tertullian (c. AD 160–225) and others, is "three persons in one essence."

All Christian traditions believe that Jesus of Nazareth is God's gift of salvation to and for the human race. Even further, all Christians would agree that belief in God should manifest in given actions and life values. But inside the Christian household—that is, within Christendom itself—there are nuanced positions on certain matters, and one of those has been the understanding of the person and work of the Holy Spirit.

Most Protestants do not believe the work of the Spirit is limited to or constrained by the Church. Paul Tillich (1886–1965) taught that the *freedom of the Holy Spirit* is *the* Protestant principle;[1] this sets a Protestant understanding of the Holy Spirit apart from older Christian communities. Tillich meant that God's Spirit works *consistently* through the witness of Christians, through the preaching of the gospel, and through believers' loving service and ministry; but *he is not bound* to work through those. He is free to do what he wants when and where he wants. The Spirit is like the wind (Jn. 3:6–8). We can see the effects of the wind, but we cannot always see where it is coming from, where it is going, or how it accomplishes what it does. Similarly, in the

Protestant understanding the Spirit is not bound to work only in the Church.

By way of contrast, Christian sacramental traditions like the Eastern Orthodox (e.g., Greeks, Russians, Ukrainians, Romanians, and so on) and the Roman Catholics believe God has sovereignly—of his own power and volition—determined that the Holy Spirit will accomplish the divine purposes through consecrated church priests, recognized church officials, and the sacraments (the Orthodox call these latter the mysteries; *sacramentum* is the Latin translation of the Greek word *mysterion*). After all, sacramentalists argue, Jesus gave his disciples authority. That authority was wed to the coming of God's Spirit in and through God-chosen appointed means: church servants, church officials, and the sacramental system.

When we read Cyprian of Carthage, who said in the third century that "there is no salvation outside the Church," and when we hear the Eastern Orthodox assert that "outside the Church there is no salvation, because salvation is the Church,"[2] we are encountering a sacramental belief system about the way God's Spirit has deemed to accomplish his purposes and cast his grace around the world. The Protestant, Roman Catholic, and Eastern Orthodox traditions each variously interpret the Bible, historical influences, and Church tradition differently from one another—and thus differ concerning the work and person of the Holy Spirit—even as they agree together that Jesus Christ is God's saving grace for all who will believe. While there are indeed Protestant traditions that are sacramental in orientation (e.g., the Reformed, Lutherans), Protestant theology as a whole does not bind the Spirit's operations to the sacraments.

The chief purpose in this book is to look at what leading Protestant theologians have taught about the Holy Spirit. Particularly, the book will highlight what different theologians have said that makes their positions unique and memorable. Finer points of thought, together with most of the intramural theological debates, can remain topics for the reader's own further study.

A theologian myself, I believe specificity and nuance of thought is of great importance. If "the devil is in the details," so also are the beauty, truth, and meaning of an idea or position. I tire of those who only want to know, "What does it mean for me?" as though truth were only a private matter. So we will try to be as specific— and meaningful—as possible on given positions without exhausting these theologians on every point concerning the Holy Spirit.

Readers will also want to know that the task of this book is primarily descriptive rather than analytical. Occasionally I will offer some analysis for further understanding of a specific point, but the central purpose is not to critique theologians or compare them one with another. As the ideas and positions become more complex through the progression of chapters, I will offer additional analysis and critique for the sake of further clarification. The reader will observe that some theologians were unmistakably influenced by prior theologians, but that does not necessarily suggest agreement or mutually accepted premises.

Rather than covering all the important Protestant theologians who have written on God's Spirit, we will survey Lutheran, Anabaptist, Anglican, Reformed, and Charismatic theologians. This will provide a good and broad sense of what Protestants have emphasized about the Spirit, and it will help us understand why whole denominations and global movements today take the specific positions that they do about the role and work of the Holy Spirit.

A quick scan of the table of contents reveals that six of our eleven theologians are from the twentieth century. Why is that? Am I privileging contemporary theologians over those of the past? No. Are contemporaries more astute than theologians in previous centuries? No. The truth is, reflection and study about the Holy Spirit is, at least in Western Christianity, a recent phenomenon. For nineteen centuries, theological emphases have rotated between Jesus as God and Savior and the Father as Creator and God. The Spirit is still, staggeringly, the most neglected member of the Trinity. Because a veritable explosion on the person and work of the Holy Spirit occurred in the twentieth century, the majority of the book will focus on that time period.

Alongside the study of a particular theologian, we will explore related areas. First, the historical context of each respective theologian will be brought to bear. Theology, which is never done in a vacuum, is always practiced in light of the pressing questions of philosophy, societal needs, and new academic insights occurring in and around it. Recognizing that theology is always contextual is important: only God's perspective is perfect and final. While we aim to see and hear God's will and purpose in a given era, we always recognize that our discernment is opaque. Saint Paul himself said, "For now we see in a mirror dimly, but then face to face; now I know in part, but then I shall know fully just as I also have been fully known" (1 Cor. 13:12).[3] During his ministry on earth Jesus said that the kingdom of God is like yeast; similarly, we might understand

God's kingdom as penetrating a given historical-cultural loaf of bread and changing it. And sure enough, history has both weighed on and been shaped by the theologies we will examine. To press this contextual point further, believers today are shaped in important ways in light of past theological teachings. In studying past and present theologians, we may understand more clearly our own churches and their theologies.

Another secondary area this book will explore is the abiding influence each theologian's position on the Holy Spirit has had in the Church. Churches and denominations today take specific emphases, tasks, and focuses often due to significant theologians. Or, in the case of the twentieth-century theologians we will examine, we will ask how those theological teachings either harmonize with the broader cultural shifts or are causing those shifts. Theologians are often accused of sitting in ivory towers and postulating arcane and spiritual matters while the *real business* of life is conducted by down-to-earth, sensible people. Yet every single one of these eleven theologians in this book cared, or today cares, passionately about how Christians live their lives. They earnestly desired that the ideas and commitments they passed along to their students and adherents make a real-life difference. In some instances, we will see that several of our twentieth-century theologians even desired theology to make a difference outside of the Church.

Jesus said he gives water that quenches the deepest human thirst (Jn. 4:4–24). That water is the Holy Spirit. May each reader find her or his thirst quenched by the surprising and playful movements of God's life-giving Spirit.

Veni, creator Spiritus! Come, Holy Spirit, come!

The Spirit Unfettered

1
Martin Luther
(1483–1546)

ON ALL HALLOWS' EVE in 1517 the Protestant Reformation erupted. A Roman Catholic monk named Martin Luther nailed ninety-five arguments, more famously called theses, on the church door in Wittenberg, Germany. In his ninety-five arguments Luther was challenging both the Church's practice of confessing sins to priests and its authority to sell indulgences: lay people would donate monetary gifts, and the Church would issue statements of forgiveness for sins. Some clerics taught that the Church's authority on this was so great that punishments in purgatory would even be shortened by ecclesiastical pronouncement. The practice of buying and selling indulgences threatened biblical teaching on salvation, reasoned Luther. A priest can pray for sinners but cannot play God concerning forgiveness.

Many previous reform-minded Roman Catholics had protested these kinds of abuses, but Luther was unique. A combination of several key factors enabled Luther's eventual tremendous impact. First, there was his training. An Augustinian monk, he understood well the life, rhythms, and teachings of Catholicism. This same perspective later served as the foil against which he would argue in his own theological writings. Luther also had the benefit of a university education, even as he initially left the academy for what he desired: his hunger for God. Second, there was his character. Luther enjoyed the fray of a good intellectual battle. Dangerous times require courageous hearts, and with the challenge of reforming long-established positions on salvation, Luther was courageous indeed.

A third key in Luther's impact was his relationships. Luther benefited from the patronage of a German prince, Frederick the Wise. Prince Frederick protected Luther from enemies who wanted to physically hurt him. Then, and also today, the help of friends in high places can offer strength to a noble cause. Fourth, originally built around AD 1440 by Johannes Gutenberg, the printing press enabled the quick spread of Luther's ideas to a European population hungry for ecclesial, political, and economic change. Luther's sermons, lectures, biblical expositions, and pamphlets made a deep impression on civil leaders, priests, and laity who wanted doctrinal clarity in their own Christian lives and churches.

Luther, like the other theologians surveyed in this book, never wrote in a historical vacuum. Roman Catholic tradition was deeply ensconced in the collective consciousness of Western Europe. Pope Gregory the Great (AD 540–604) declared that God's grace, if it is to be effective in this life, needs human beings' active participation through deeds of love and repentance. In short, Luther was challenging traditions that were nearly a millennium old. This means that the doctrinal stakes, and with them political stakes, were incredibly high: how should authority in Christian life and thought be construed and understood? Should the wisdom of tradition simply be jettisoned in light of new biblical-interpretive insights? Just who gets to authoritatively interpret the Bible? Answers to those questions determine answers to questions such as, on what basis can one have God's salvation? and, who is *damned*? Again, the historical context weighed heavily on Luther as he studied, thought, and taught about the Holy Spirit.

While Luther did not write a lengthy book on the Holy Spirit, including his work on God's Spirit in this study is essential because Luther is such a foundational theologian for later Protestantism. Therefore, we must understand what Luther believed and taught. Among theologians Luther gives us a baseline, a starting place, for understanding subsequent developments. In fact, one prominent monograph suggests Luther's theology of the Holy Spirit was a key ingredient that informed all his many reflections.[4] With that in mind, we will look at the place and function of the Holy Spirit in some of Luther's doctrines that profoundly shaped Protestantism: namely, his understandings of human nature, of God's revelation, and of the sign of God's presence.

THE HOLY SPIRIT

To understand Luther let's examine the position he rejected. Medieval Catholic theology had, in Luther's estimation, too optimistic a view of human nature. Yes, the Bible reveals that humankind is both "a little lower than the angels" (Ps. 8:5;

Heb. 2:7) and of all God's creatures is alone created in God's image (Gen. 1:26). But for Luther the consistent biblical emphasis falls rather on humankind's sinfulness. Medieval Roman Catholic teaching held that humankind consisted of both a lower and a higher nature. The lower sensual nature (flesh) was understood to be a key location for human sinfulness, with the appetites for food and sex residing in this lower nature. This element of humanity tended to pull people down toward sin or be targeted by evil for sin. The higher spiritual nature (spirit), however, was created by God as the dimension of human existence where the Spirit of God made contact with people. For example, in the fifth century Saint Augustine (AD 354–430) had famously said, "Our hearts are restless until they rest in thee." Whether Augustine was merely speaking poetically about his own hunger for God or whether he was expressing a foundational philosophical truth about the inner workings of human nature is debatable. What is clear is that for many centuries Greek philosophical reflection mixed with both the biblical passages on human nature and traditional Catholic teachings like those of Augustine and his later medieval interpreters. This resulted in a belief that God's grace, through the work of the Holy Spirit, builds on human nature and perfects it. In short, the Roman Catholic theology of Luther's day did not believe human beings could save themselves; but it was an optimistic understanding of humanity in that it espoused that our higher nature naturally hungers for transcendence (see Glossary). Regin Prenter's book on Luther and the Holy Spirit summarizes this medieval position: "Grace [was] the God-given power to strive forward and upward to the distant goal of salvation."[5]

For Luther the medieval Catholic understanding of the Spirit and God's grace was gravely erroneous. Committed as he was to both the veracity of God's revelatory acts in history and the Bible as the final doctrinal authority, Luther was little interested in the philosophical commitments of traditional Catholic positions (even as his own method of biblical interpretation was informed by certain philosophical commitments). Luther adamantly asserted that true Christian teaching was that the whole of human nature was utterly and totally depraved and that God stands in judgment over the whole of human nature. Even our intellect has been blinded by sin. Rather than pursue God in our hearts, we naturally tend toward self-deception and self-protection. Indeed, Luther argued sin resides in the self-will, a capacity understood by medieval Roman Catholics to be situated in the higher or spiritual element of human nature. There is nothing, Luther insisted, we can do to save ourselves: we stand under the wrath of a righteous God.

It is Luther's position on human nature and salvation, however, that reveals his theology about the Holy Spirit. Luther understood that God sends his Spirit to redeem the whole person. Salvation is by faith alone (*sola fide*)—a key Reformation maxim.[6] However, faith itself is only possible by the work of the Holy Spirit—an important understanding for Luther. God is the first mover; we can do absolutely nothing to approach him unless God first sends his Spirit to convict us of sin and to give us the gift of faith.

Luther reasoned that this God-first dynamic rules out all manner of works righteousness. Not only can we not reach out to God on our own, we would not even know our need to pursue God unless he first came to us. We can do nothing to earn our salvation. We can do nothing to make ourselves more righteous. We are doomed. God's righteousness is alien: it exists outside of us entirely and comes to us by the Spirit as the gift of God through Jesus Christ. Internally we are utterly sinful, but Christ's righteousness is reckoned unto us by the grace of God (Rom. 4:4–6). In his *Small Catechism* Luther wrote, " 'Why is it necessary that the Holy Ghost work this faith in you?' The Holy Ghost does this for us when we are *'spiritually blind, dead*, and an *enemy of God,'* when we cannot come by our own reason or strength to believe in Jesus Christ or to come to him."[7] The Spirit then, for Luther, is the person of God who comes to us to enable faith. Salvation is impossible apart from God's Spirit.

Luther's view of the human person, together with his view of salvation, substantially challenged Roman Catholic doctrine. This did not, however, cause Luther to jettison all of Catholic tradition. Not only did he believe there was wisdom to be gained from earlier theologians like Augustine; he also maintained the doctrine of sacraments, albeit in a modified way.[8] Roman Catholicism generally held to seven sacraments. Luther, owing to his biblical interpretation, argued for only two: water baptism and the Lord's Supper. These two were specifically instituted by Christ, and for Luther the Christological moorings of Christianity were foundational. Moreover, it was his conviction that the whole of Scripture, breathed as it was of the Holy Spirit, found its center in Christ. It was through Christ that the Spirit came for our benefit.

The connection between the Holy Spirit and Jesus Christ was integral for Luther's theology. In the New Testament, per Jesus and the apostles, the Spirit comes to redeem people *only* on the basis of Jesus Christ's person and work. Following the broad sweep of the New Testament, Luther held that the persons of the Godhead are inseparable. "In the beginning was the Word, and the Word was with God, and the Word was God," said John the Evangelist in 1:1 of his Gospel. The Word, who was eternally God, was somehow distinct from God the Father; yet they were inseparably united. Later, in John 15:26, Jesus taught that when God's Spirit comes later he will bear witness to Jesus. Theology building on ancient Church councils like Nicea (AD 325) asserted that the persons of the Godhead always work in concert. Luther entirely affirmed that.

Where the Word, second person of the Trinity, abides there will the Spirit also abide. Where the Spirit is at work, he is at work in and only through the W/word (*Word* capitalized refers to the incarnate Christ; *word* lowercased indicates other expressions of God's revelation.) In Luther's theology the Spirit always dynamically accompanies God's revelation, God's word, whether incarnate—enfleshed as Jesus Christ—written, or preached. God's Word has power: he created the universe by speaking (Gen. 1). Jesus, the preeminent Word of God, had power: he spoke and demons' mouths shut; Jesus spoke and blind eyes were opened. The written word too, spiritually and existentially enlivened by the Spirit, has power. Jesus proclaimed this, saying, "Man shall not live on bread alone, but on every word that proceeds from the mouth of God" (Mt. 4:4). The preached word is power, "The power of God for salvation to everyone who believes" (Rom. 1:16).

This coworking of the Word and Spirit did not mean for Luther that a mere mechanical or uninvolved preaching of the word would cause change in people's hearts. Woodenly and ritualistically serving the sacraments would not necessitate effective regeneration by the Spirit. For Luther faith remains operative and key to the transformative process. The apostle Paul had said, "Faith comes from hearing, and hearing by the word of Christ" (Rom. 10:17). Elsewhere Paul taught about the Spirit's faith-giving role, "No one can say, 'Jesus is Lord,' except by the Holy Spirit" (1 Cor. 12:3). Given his dynamic Word-Spirit dual-working theology, we can thus see why Luther so emphasized preaching the gospel. A tremendous Reformation outcome, across all of Roman Catholic and Protestant Western Europe, was a renewed emphasis on preaching.

Important to this Word-Spirit dynamic for Luther was that the Word always came forth from God first; the Word always has primacy before the Spirit. Luther believed this was the biblical pattern, the biblical teaching: the Word is first and then Spirit. God's word is uttered, and the Spirit immediately descends on and through that word. Describing Luther's position, Prenter says, "Where the Word is, the Spirit inevitably soon follows. But the Spirit does not come before the Word has preceded it. It is not without significance to note that this order cannot be changed. It is always first the outward Word and then— soon—the Spirit with the inner Word."[9] The Spirit works through God-ordained means: Scripture, Jesus of Nazareth, the preached gospel, and the sacraments. The Spirit is free as God to redeem those whom he pleases—Jesus declared in John 3:8, "The wind blows where it wishes . . . so is everyone who is born of the Spirit." Yet the Spirit does not work apart from the expression of God's word. Luther was too strongly committed to both the biblical pattern of the Word and Spirit's coworking and the ancient Church's confessional Trinitarian formulas like Nicea and Constantinople, "three persons in one essence," to allow that one person of the Trinity ever worked apart from the other persons.

Similarly, sacraments are Christ-instituted means by which believers encounter God's grace. The sacraments—rituals involving physical means—accord with God's having revealed himself in history. Just as Christ appeared in history by the Spirit (the Holy Spirit overshadowed Mary and she became pregnant with Jesus, Lk. 1:35), and just as Christ's saving work was manifested in history in the Holy Spirit (Jesus said he was working by the power of God's Spirit, Matt. 12:28), so also sacraments serve as Spirit-given vehicles for God to meet believers in time and space. Jesus is not a mere ancient ethical idea to be mimicked. The gospel is not a message from outer space to deliver us to a spiritual realm. Instead, with Luther, an in-this-world quality to God's revelation was effected, and continues to be effective, in time and space—in and through the sacraments—for those with faith.[10] God meets us where we are: this is beautiful! In the sacraments God meets us *who* we are! Yet through the sacraments God's Spirit works to save us and transform our nature.

Luther affirmed that the Bible teaches God's Spirit is the source of all life (Gen. 1:2; 2:7; 6:17; 7:15, 22; 2 Cor. 3:17–18). And, because the Spirit is God, the Spirit is therefore omnipresent. The Spirit's omnipresence does not mean though that wherever the Spirit as Creator is present that people are therefore regenerate or redeemed. Life is given by the Spirit, but life is perpetually corrupted by sin. There is a restorative and regenerative work that the Spirit seeks to pour into sinful people. However, the Spirit exclusively works toward redemption through God's W/word; Luther thus made a distinction between the Spirit's original gift of life and the subsequent regenerative gift. This distinction between physical life and regenerated life will be at issue especially for later theologians and their reflections on the Spirit's omnipresence.

Currently in society there are battles about the reliability of all truth claims. The reliability of a truth claim also concerned people in the sixteenth century who thought that there should be some kind of proof of, or some way to measure, true Christianity. Some Christians variously argued that mystical experiences, holy states of being, or upright moral lives were proof of the Spirit's presence. While Luther did not speak against any of those things, he adamantly affirmed that we only know Christ by faith. "It is God who does his work in us, not we who imitate Christ," Prenter says, summarizing Luther. "Conformity with the will of God is the work of the Spirit, not the result of the struggling of the will."[11] God's Spirit works first, and we respond to the Spirit's work. Spiritual experiences or upright attitudes derive from various causes and explanations. So also one's lifestyle; a multiplicity of reasons drives one to act in what appear to be morally upright ways: self-righteousness, appearing "spiritual" to others, an unquestioned obedience to legal codes, even doctrinal dogmatism. "Our being in Christ is finally a matter of faith, not of visions and raptures," says Donald Bloesch, echoing Luther.[12]

Sanctification, a process of constant regeneration in Luther's theology, is ongoing throughout life and never complete. The reality of Christ in a believer's life for Luther is found in God's word (Christ, Scripture, the preached gospel), rather than our feelings. We can learn obedience and love of Christ through our experiences, but our heart's final measure is God. Indeed, the one who believes in Christ *will* experience the Spirit's presence, but that experience is never the measurement of one's walk with Christ. This means that in Luther's theology the subjective or existential proof of one's Christian commitment is vague. "In Luther," says Prenter, "empirical piety is always ambiguous. It may in every moment be either an expression of the Spirit or of the flesh, according to whether the man in that particular moment is either Spirit or flesh. Therefore it is impossible to speak of an unambiguous growth in the plan of real justification."[13] Growth in piety is the fruit of the Spirit, but such growth is not itself proof of regeneration. In later chapters we will witness how other theologians have found this tension unbearable.

Rather paradoxically, inner turmoil concerning sin signifies the Spirit's presence for Luther. A believer is invaded by Christ's alien righteousness through the Spirit, where sanctification is something God does *for us*, not something we generate by daily routine, spiritual discipline, or force of will. Luther drives this point home in his *Small Catechism*, "'What is the work of the Holy Ghost?' The Holy Ghost sanctifies me, that is, He *makes me holy*, by bringing me to faith in Christ and by imparting to me the blessings of redemption. (Sanctification in the wider sense includes everything that the Holy Ghost does in me.)"[14]

Simultaneously the believer is both a sinner and one justified in Christ (in Latin, *simul iustus et peccator*). Sin remains within the believer even though the Holy Spirit works to regenerate that believer. This conflict between sin and righteousness enflames a Christian the moment that person first believes. Luther reasoned that the apostle Paul was describing this very struggle between the Spirit and the flesh in Romans 7:8–24: a Christian is both an *old man* and a *new man* at the same time.[15] Only at the resurrection will we finally be what God wants us to be in Christ.

ABIDING INFLUENCE

Unquestionably Luther's greatest influence on theology is his doctrine of justification by faith. Today all Evangelicals (see Glossary), most Protestants, and millions of Roman Catholics agree with Luther on salvation: Christ alone is sufficient, and faith in Christ is essential. There is less agreement about Luther's theology of the Holy Spirit. Christians in other traditions have worked diligently to address the ambiguity of the Spirit's work and presence in Luther's position.

Concerning his understanding of the Spirit, Luther insisted that the Spirit comes to us as the person of God. Eastern Orthodoxy and to some extent Roman Catholicism prefer to speak of the Spirit's work in terms of uncreated energy or divine grace. Luther's biblical personalism—that God's salvific work is accomplished together in history through the persons of Christ and the Holy Spirit, for the sake of whole human selves—set Protestant hermeneutics (the study of biblical texts) on a trajectory that would reshape and reenvision vast sweeps of Christendom. Some Protestants today still speak and teach of the Spirit as an *it*, thereby depersonalizing the third member of the Trinity. Luther, rather, believed the Bible narrated encounters between human beings and the supreme being: God himself.

Luther's Word-Spirit tandem has been critical for subsequent Protestant theology. Luther insisted the Word (Christ) qualifies the Spirit as the one specifically sent by Jesus; the good news (word of God), preached by Christians, is foremost to the Spirit's work among sinners. The Holy Spirit gives physical, creaturely life (*creator Spiritus*) to all creatures, but physical life from the Spirit is not eternal life; eternal life comes from Christ alone. On this Luther mirrored older medieval Catholic theology that believed God's grace comes to enhance nature. Reigning until the twentieth century, Luther's distinctions between physical life and eternal life held fast among Protestant theology.

Even as Luther initiated substantial changes in Christian reflection and thought, not everyone found agreement with him. Still others thought he failed to push hard enough for rupture with Roman Catholicism. Among those critics were the Anabaptists. The next chapter portrays how they superseded Luther on several matters, including the doctrine of the Holy Spirit.

2
The Sixteenth-Century Anabaptists

HISTORICAL CONTEXT

ARTIN LUTHER had no initial intention of breaking entirely with either Christian tradition or the Catholic Church. What he could not foresee were the uncontrollable winds of the Reformation that, once astir, would become potent and chaotic. Powerful megaforces working simultaneously on European lands—philosophical shifts (e.g., the rise of humanism [see Glossary]), political realignments (formation of nation-states), and economic restructuring (the rise of the middle class)—combined for an era of transformation unrivaled until the twentieth century.

The sweeping spiritual and theological shifts of the sixteenth-century Reformation did not remain isolated from these larger sociocultural forces. Opportunists all across Europe, both inside and outside Roman Catholicism, eagerly used aspects of spirituality and theology to benefit themselves, their familial estates, their city-states, and their political allies. Many thought it was an exciting time to be alive, but for others life became chaotic and frightening. Many struggled to determine truth and its foundations. Leaders wondered how to achieve certainty about Christian life and faith.

One group proposing solutions was the Anabaptists: Amish, Hutterites, and Mennonites. Scattered across Europe (initially in Switzerland, Germany, the Netherlands, and Moravia), the Anabaptists were deemed radical by both Roman Catholics and Magisterial Protestants (see Glossary). Whereas most Catholic monks remained isolated within monasteries and remained single, the Anabaptists withdrew from society in communitarian fashion. They formed enclaves in towns and villages where they married and bore children. They rendered to Caesar what was owed to Caesar, but they consistently avoided participating in larger civil affairs; and many of them believed Christians ought to refrain entirely from governmental involvement.

The Anabaptists stressed simplicity, modesty, and economic frugality and became harsh critics of lending money for profit. Some sought to live radically by holding all possessions in common. Philosophically their leaders like Hans Denck (AD 1495–1527) were influenced by humanism (see Glossary), which meant they were committed to studying Scripture apart from established Roman Catholic tradition.

Because of these radical tendencies, many viewed the Anabaptists as suspect, for they challenged the long-established status quo. Indeed, the very name Anabaptist began as a term of condescension because they rebaptized newly confessing adults. Following their biblical interpretation, only those who believe and confess Christ as Lord are to be baptized, and because infants are incapable of both believing and confessing

Jesus, Anabaptists argued vehemently against infant baptism. Catholics and Protestants subsequently feared that Anabaptist ideas would destabilize not just traditional Christianity but also the entire existing social fabric.

Influential leaders of the Reformation, like Martin Luther, John Calvin, and Huldrych Zwingli, were forceful in arguing for the principle of *sola scriptura*: Scripture alone should be consulted about Christian faith and life. Despite the heated rhetoric that often accompanied Reformation debate, those three reformers remained willing to both consult and learn from the church fathers, particularly Augustine (AD 354–430), when it came to reading and understanding the biblical texts. In contrast, the Anabaptists insisted that the biblical text be taken on its own terms as a supreme authority.

Here is a simple but helpful way of understanding the Reformers' views of biblical authority:

- Lutherans did not want to do anything that was forbidden in the Bible.
- the Reformed only wanted to do what had warrant in the Bible.
- the Anabaptists discarded anything they could not find in the Bible.

Compared to other Protestants, the Anabaptists were more radical—hence the oft-used name for them—both in their reading of Scripture and in their political-economic positions.

In the Anabaptists' opinion the Roman Catholic Church for centuries allowed far too many layers of harmful silt to cover

over the plain teachings of the Bible. Addressing this state of affairs, Menno Simons (ca. AD 1496–1561), leader of the Mennonites, said about the Bible, "It is so obscured by the ugly, leavenous dung of human commands, statutes, and glosses, that scarcely one or two is found in a thousand who have caught the true sense and meaning."[16] Echoing a similar sentiment, Balthasar Hubmaier (AD 1480–1528) called Roman Catholics "heretics who cast a veil over the Scriptures and interpret them otherwise than the Holy Spirit demands."[17]

Moreover, for the Anabaptists, most of church history was devoid of the presence of the Holy Spirit. Thomas Müntzer (ca. AD 1488–1525), a German Anabaptist leader, exemplified this outlook when he wrote, "For a thousand years no man has had the Holy Spirit; the Church is not ruled by it either."[18] The Anabaptists, working harder and more resolutely at Reformation than even Martin Luther, believed they were returning believers to first-century apostolic Christianity, particularly concerning their understandings of the Holy Spirit.

THE HOLY SPIRIT

In a way frightening to other Protestants and Roman Catholics but that would become normal practice for large segments of Protestantism in Church history, the Anabaptists believed that every true Christian had the right to interpret Scripture for themselves. Anabaptists asserted the Holy Spirit came in and through the written word of God to illumine believers' hearts and minds with fresh insight into the meaning and application of biblical texts. Mennonite leader Menno Simons wrote of the

Spirit, "He guides us into all truth; He justifies us. He cleanses, sanctifies, reconciles, comforts, reproves, cheers, and assures us. He testifies with our spirit that we are the children of God."[19] As seen in this quote, the Holy Spirit was, for the Anabaptists, *the* critical component of new life in Christ. It was God's Spirit who enabled someone to believe in Christ. It was the Spirit who brought faith, strengthened obedience, and fortified those who suffered on Christ's behalf. It was the Holy Spirit that called and discipled believers to share the mutuality of Christian community. While Martin Luther and other Protestants embraced the Holy Spirit's work, they did not place the same emphasis on the Spirit as that characterized by the Anabaptists.

According to the Anabaptist tradition, farmers who had the Holy Spirit were deemed more qualified to interpret and understand the Bible than either unregenerate Catholic priests or unregenerate theologians. This was because for Anabaptists it was the Spirit that gave Scripture its authority. The Holy Spirit authored Scripture and was the true interpreter of Scripture. Those who had the Spirit, then, were more qualified to interpret the Bible than those who did not. They believed it possible to read and understand the Bible with one's mind but not be convicted, strengthened, or assured in the inner person. The Holy Spirit, Anabaptists insisted, comes and illumines God's written word so that it becomes a powerful and living dynamic. Their openness to the Spirit's illumination and guidance also saw Anabaptists embrace charismatic gifts like prophecy, speaking in tongues, and miracles, even as the emphasis in Anabaptism consistently fell toward Christian character and ethical living rather than the more spectacular spiritual gifts.

Soon, however, Anabaptists' sometimes-subjectivist method of biblical interpretation began to produce problems. There was the unfortunate instance of the Mennonite Jan of Leiden (in Münster), who in 1534, claimed he had new revelations from God, reintroduced the Old Testament practice of polygamy, and began to call himself "King David." Other Anabaptists, based on their own reading of the Bible, rejected one or both of the doctrines of Christ's divinity and the Trinity.[20] Quickly, however, several Anabaptist leaders realized that a baldly subjectivist (private) reading of the Bible had dangers; they went on to counsel that the entire Christian community, thus involving more carefully trained leaders, needed to be taught basics in biblical interpretation. This involvement of the larger community, creating checks and balances, enabled the Anabaptist tradition to maintain a healthy integrative tension between God's word—that is, the Bible—and God's Spirit.[21] Indeed, even cursory studies of historic Anabaptist writings reveal that they consistently wrote about the Holy Spirit with nearly incessant Scripture references.

The Anabaptists did not believe the Holy Spirit is bound to the Roman Catholic Mass or the sacramental system. Catholicism for centuries asserted that Jesus had given the church the power and authority to dispense the grace of God;[22] the Mass and in particular the Eucharist were held to be God-ordained means of grace. A common perception held in Roman Catholic tradition was that the more one received the Eucharist the more likely it was that one would go to heaven. Grace, viewed by many Europeans prior to the Reformation, was a spiritual-physical substance that could be transmitted through physical means—the sacraments. Luther believed grace came through the two sacraments—water baptism and the Lord's Supper—but only when faith was present in the believer. In contrast to both Catholics and Luther, the Anabaptists variously saw those ceremonies as memorials of Christ's person and work and as commandments to be obeyed by the Christian community rather than as sacraments used by the Holy Spirit to convey grace. Again, the Anabaptists espoused more extreme positions, even concerning traditional sacramental doctrine.

A particularly explosive component of Anabaptist thought was that the "false" ritualism of the Catholics created a hindrance to true Christian piety. Menno Simons wrote about the difficulty of finding true religion. Instead, he discovered, "Everywhere nothing but ugly, erring unbelief and undisciplined carnal life; false doctrine, falsely adorned sacraments, a satanic heart and mind, an accursed, heathenish idolatry under Christ's name."[23] In some respects, the Anabaptists were not only against formalism (adhering to prescribed and fixed Christian forms), but against form. Their tradition became characterized by a more free-flowing existence, and not only concerning religion—but, as noted earlier, of distinctions on government, economics, community, and Bible reading. Among their differently held beliefs, they also opposed both the formulation of creeds (see Glossary) and writings they perceived to be staunchly dogmatic in content.

Making the Anabaptists unique was their view that the Holy Spirit enables believers to live in the freedom of Christ and rise above religious legalism. Following Jesus for them was not a matter of keeping rules or simple adherence to an accepted body of truths. Christianity was life—transforming life. German Anabaptist leader Hans Denck wrote, "Whoever has received God's new covenant, that is whoever has had the law written into his heart by the Holy Spirit, is truly righteous. Whoever thinks he can observe the law by means of the Book ascribes to the dead letter what belongs to the living Spirit."[24] The Spirit approaches not to promote strict adherence to tradition but to transform the person into the image of Christ. To this end the Anabaptists transformed Roman Catholicism's "three sacraments of baptism, penance, and extreme unction" into "three actions of grace: adult repentance, a life of contrition and penitential suffering, and the benediction of martyrdom." "All three acts were called baptisms." And each of these baptisms had as its goal the believer's transformation.[25]

In light of Church history, Anabaptists' emphasis on *lived* and experiential Christianity was not a new position. For centuries many Roman Catholic theologians and monks had averred the same; notably Francis of Assisi (AD 1181/2–1226), Catherine of Siena (AD 1347–80), and Thomas à Kempis (c. AD 1380–1471). So, while the Anabaptists forcefully broke from the Roman Catholic institution, they were nevertheless promoting spiritual avenues long accepted by devout Catholics. Again, the Anabaptists were unique because they unfettered the Holy Spirit from the institutional Church.

Also like the Catholics, but distinct from Luther and Calvin, the Anabaptists taught that the believer must cooperate with the Holy Spirit's illumination and grace if transformation is to occur. Denck typified this when he wrote, "This [perfection of the Spirit] is the one aim toward which all who are being saved should seek. Only to the extent that one beholds the perfection of the Spirit is one saved. The closer one comes to it, the farther one is from condemnation."[26] Theologians call this cooperation synergism: the work of God together with the person's work. (Today Protestants vary on the role and place of synergism in the doctrines of salvation and sanctification—becoming like Christ).

ABIDING INFLUENCE

Within contemporary evangelical Protestantism we witness Anabaptist influence in several ways: (1) emphasis on Christian life as being in God's Spirit; (2) an embrace of *sola scriptura*; (3) holding to subjectivist (privatized) tendencies in Christian teachings and life; (4) restorationist impulses: the attempt to return to biblical or apostolic Christianity, however that is understood; and (5) disdain for Church history in general and Christian tradition in particular. Each of those five deserves further nuance.

Christian life is something lived in God's Spirit: Anabaptist teaching is replicated when Pentecostals (see Glossary) and Charismatics (see Glossary) make the Holy Spirit central to being Christian. This does not mean Pentecostals or Charismatics were immediately influenced by Anabaptism; after all, Pentecostalism and the Charismatic movement arose in the twentieth century. However, Anabaptists elevated the prominence of the Spirit first; centuries later—when Protestantism spread globally and many Protestant traditions crossfertilized one another around the world via revival meetings, shared mission enterprises, and widely disseminated devotional publications and academic textbooks in the nineteenth and twentieth centuries—the Anabaptist emphasis on the Spirit abounded. Among the globe's nearly 600 million Pentecostals, it is widely celebrated today that all Christians—not just pastors, clerics, nuns, or monks—may profoundly experience the Spirit.

In the twenty-first century most Protestants see Scripture as the supreme authority for matters of Christian life and faith. Very few Protestant denominations practice a stark principle of *sola scriptura* because through the course of decades and centuries each denomination has developed a guiding interpretive tradition. However, especially among low-church and free-church Protestants—who variously have pastors and not priests, baptize adults but not infants, and see the Lord's Supper and water baptism as ordinances commanded by Jesus rather than sacraments—Anabaptism's commitment to the authority of Scripture is clearly influential. Not the Church but the Bible is, among low-church and free-church Protestants, *the* Christian storehouse of authoritative tradition. Individual believers are encouraged to seek God's Spirit within the biblical text.

Subjectivist (privatized) tendencies are soaring within Christendom. A multitude of historical influences have caused the rise of subjective manifestations of Christian experience and doctrine, and not all those causes have Christian moorings (e.g., existential philosophy and economic globalization, both of which powerfully transmit Western individualism). Nevertheless, the Anabaptists imported the preexisting Catholic teachings of encounter with Christ through the Spirit, making them normative for generations of Protestant believers around the world.

Another Anabaptist influence, restorationism, the desire to return to what the first-century apostolic community experienced, has existed within many sects and Catholic monastic movements across Christianity's two-thousand-year history. The Anabaptists desired to return to the apostles' experience of the Spirit's presence. Other radical sixteenth-century Protestant reform movements (current historians group them under "spiritualism")[27] took antiformal, antihistorical, and antistructural cues from Anabaptists, carrying their spiritualist teachings to extremes: the Holy Spirit might trump the teachings of the Bible with new revelations; the Holy Spirit is existent in all people, not just Christians; Christian life is about experience, not widely embraced truth or teachings; there is no need for organized churches. Anabaptists are exempt from most of those positions, but in fascinating ways Anabaptists both engaged communal approaches and celebrated experiential Christianity that facilitated those extremes.

The Anabaptists' yearnings for a thoroughgoing Christian lifestyle were not unique. Prior centuries of monasteries' works and contributions to society attest the same. Yet not all Protestants believed vast swaths of historic Christian tradition and teaching needed to be rejected for the sake of revitalization. One leader who sought a middle ground between old Church teachings and new movements of God was the Anglican John Wesley, the missionary-turned-evangelist who is the next chapter's focus.

3
John Wesley
(1703–91)

*I*N 1735 JOHN WESLEY sailed from his home in Britain to the North American colony of Georgia to missionize Native Americans. By that year the Reformation was already some 220 years old. Although a small number of Protestant denominations had been founded from the outset, now there were a great deal more, indicating that there were more, not less, questions that Christian leaders and theologians needed to navigate. Moreover, existing Protestant traditions and denominations had become characterized by internal distinctions. This meant that Wesley, living in a pluralist Christian context, had both opportunity and necessity to mine many traditions and teachings for his own ministry.

Raised an Anglican, Wesley inhabited a tradition renowned for being a *via media*, a middle way between Roman Catholicism and Protestantism. The Anglicans on the one hand shared Catholic interest in church doctrine and structure, and on the other hand emphasized faith in their theology, like the Protestants, particularly concerning the doctrine of salvation. Anglicans held

.

a person was justified by faith in Jesus Christ apart from works and that one encountered God's grace through sacraments served by consecrated priests.

Educated at Oxford, Wesley continued his education by reading studiously throughout his life. His love of learning facilitated his familiarity with the era's cutting-edge scientific and philosophical questions. With a voracious intellectual curiosity he learned from the whole Church—Roman Catholics, Eastern Orthodox, Magisterial Reformers (see Glossary), and Pietists (see Glossary). How Christians should live—Christianity as a lived experience—especially concerned Wesley. His desire as a minister was to cure souls, something he called "practical divinity." It follows that when Wesley wrote about Christian life, the Holy Spirit was a less speculative or academic matter and more one of daily life in Christ. His interest in Christianity as an experience, and not just a body of doctrine, marks him as one of the founders of modern day Evangelicalism (see Glossary).

THE HOLY SPIRIT

Across his lifetime Wesley anchored his theology of the Holy Spirit in his doctrine of salvation, preserving the Reformation's earlier emphasis. He charted the Holy Spirit's involvement in drawing us to salvation, convicting us of sin, and sanctifying us. Specifically, throughout Wesley's teaching we see an over-arching concern with holiness and love. Wesley believed the Scriptures teach that God is a being of holiness and love. God's own character is normative for ours, and Wesley taught that

Christians should ache to replicate God's holiness and love in their daily lives.

Since God's character is archetypal for Christian character, Wesley knew God's identity needed clear description. God's two chief attributes—holiness and love—inform and characterize one another, Wesley adamantly insisted. Holiness never exists alone in God, and love never exists in God without holiness. If God were primarily love, as some ministers and professors argued, God himself would be sentimental and love would be self-indulgent. If God were primarily holiness, God's judgment would consume us without compassion. Instead, for Wesley, God's love is holy and pure, and God's holiness is directed toward loving relationship.[28]

This God of holy love, Wesley asserted, created human beings in his image; that is, they were initially characterized by both holiness and love. Detailed in understanding, Wesley believed the *imago Dei*, the image of God, consisted of three elements: the natural image, the political image, and the moral image. The *natural image* pertains to our being. Embodied spirits, we are both physical and spiritual, but it is the spiritual that makes us unique among God's earthly creations, even as our capacities to understand and choose are wed to the natural image. Despite the fall in Eden the natural image abides, albeit corrupted and perverted; our understanding is always clouded, our choosing is consistently corrupted, and our bodies are wracked with death.

The second image, the *political image*, for Wesley, expresses our relation to physical nature and other creatures. God gave us dominion over the animals, making us to be "lord of this lower creation."[29] In so doing God shared his rule with people. We were meant to bless nature with dignity and respect as God's good creation. Theologian Kenneth Collins summarizes Wesley's understanding of the political image, "The grace of God then often bears a human face."[30] Our own brutality to the created order witnesses that the political image has been obscured; instead of being a blessing to creation we are now a curse.

The third image, the *moral image*, is the lynchpin for understanding Wesley on both his doctrine of humanity and the Holy Spirit's work. Of Wesley's three categories we are closest to God's nature concerning the moral image. The moral image gave us capacity to worship and know God and also formed the context for our potential sin. In short, the moral image put us in relationship to and with God. And God's holy love extended to us through this moral image. We were created to love God in holy fashion, with purity of heart and moral righteousness. While morality did not form the basis of the divine-human relationship, it was critical in giving that relationship integrity.

Wesley, following the path of Augustine and Luther, maintained a doctrine of total depravity. However, whereas Luther held tightly to an understanding of devastation of God's image in human beings, Wesley believed it was primarily the moral image that was depraved. Satan fell from God through pride, but Adam and Eve fell through unbelief. That element of their nature enabling their right relationship with God—the moral image—was totally ruined and lost. Wesley said, "the life of God was extinguished in [Adam's] soul. The glory departed from him. He lost the whole moral image of God, righteousness and true holiness. He was unholy; he was unhappy; he was full of sin, full of guilt and tormenting fears."[31] Left to ourselves,

Wesley maintained, we are doomed to death and alienation.
Our whole God-given orientation in life was twisted and
perverted. In Wesley's terrifying understanding of the Fall and
of sin, our very attitudes and dispositions toward life and God
were redirected and befouled. Adam and Eve, says Collins,
"were unhappy precisely because they were unholy."[32]

Totally depraved. Nothing we can do bridges the gap
between ourselves and God. Nothing we can do heals the
pervasive wound in our souls. Nothing we do by ourselves stops
our proclivity to sin.

Thank God for Jesus Christ and his Spirit—Wesley, following Augustine's lead, taught a unique doctrine called prevenient
grace. Whereas Augustine and Luther accounted for the salvation of believers through the doctrine of predestination—God's
mysterious choosing, from before creation, to save some—
Wesley for his part took a more nuanced (though some in the
Augustinian tradition might say a less committed) position. He
believed that Christ Jesus' person and work make possible the
Holy Spirit's coming to sinners and moving in their hearts. God
did not arbitrarily decide to save some before time, as Augustine
and Luther argued. Instead, Wesley taught, God convicts of sin
and brings saving faith—in the here and now. Significantly,
Wesley rooted this doctrine in John 1:9, "There was the true
light which, coming into the world, enlightens every man." The
Spirit, Wesley taught, approaches sinners and awakens them to
their sinfulness, begins to work on their hearts so they desire to
please God, thus moving them toward salvation.

Salvation is completely by grace, Wesley maintained; he
stood in good Protestant tradition with this assertion. Not only

can we not save ourselves, we cannot even desire salvation apart from the initial work of God's prodding Spirit. The Spirit first comes to us, but we are not saved simply through the Spirit's movement on our hearts. God moves first—this is prevenient grace—but we must respond or salvation is impossible.

Wesley held that there are several benefits of prevenient grace:

1. Unlike something people deduce from observation, God in his grace toward sinners has granted all people a basic knowledge of the existence of God and his attributes.

2. Despite the obfuscation of original sin we still know right from wrong due to a post-Fall rewriting of the moral law on human hearts. (Wesley did not clarify how this occurred in history.) Thus, God has given all human beings a conscience. From the Latin word meaning, "with knowledge," conscience is the innate capacity whereby we know right from wrong. By this we know that God loves his creation and did not abandon it to wanton immoral destruction.

3. A measure of free will—the ability to choose good over evil—given by the Holy Spirit, resides within sinners. Since Wesley held that free will was ruined in the Fall, this is a fascinating tension in his theology. As with conscience, free will might be replenished by God, by his own grace, in sinners. Apart from God's grace, a sinner's will can only choose evil.

4. A cumulative effect, Wesley argued, regarding the previously enumerated three godly benefits places a brake or a check on human wickedness and perversity within

society.[33] If one were to ask Wesley, "Why do sinners still do good deeds?" or, "Given our tendency to destruction, why is it that the human race hasn't annihilated itself?" he would undoubtedly answer, "Because of God's prevenient grace."

Following the moment of salvation, that moment when a person is restored to right relationship with God through Jesus Christ, a moment (and a process) Wesley sometimes called regeneration or justification, the Holy Spirit works in the believers' hearts to transform them. This transformation speaks into a second distinctive teaching in Wesley's theology: sanctification.

Because the tendency to sin abides in Christians all their lives, believers are at the same time righteous and sinful people; on this matter Wesley agreed with Luther's *simul iustus et peccator*. Christians are forgiven, but that does not stop their sinning. Nevertheless, the Holy Spirit moves in believers' hearts to uproot willful sinning and to steadily transform them into Christ's image. The Spirit's transforming grace may be resisted by believers who choose darkness over the light, but the Spirit's perpetual flood of grace in a believer will eventually produce sanctification. An inward change of heart, Wesley asserted, will produce an outward change of lifestyle.

Especially attributed to Wesley is the notion that the Spirit comes with God's holy love to transform a Christian's dispositions (feelings and tendencies), attitudes, and appetites. Christians are not merely saved, if by salvation we mean simply forgiven by God. Yes, Christians are dramatically changed in a conversion moment; but they are also changed gradually, so that their willing and feelings align with Christ. Wesley believed Christians should have a certain correspondence to the way Christ himself would have *felt*, *responded*, and *navigated* daily life. Christians should be thoroughly like Jesus if they truly walk in the Spirit. Whereas when a sinner might respond to situations with pride, selfishness, or love of the world, a sanctified believer will respond with humility, service to others, and love of God.

This growth in Christlikeness is accompanied by growth in assurance of one's salvation. Wesley, like Luther and Calvin, would not allow subjectivity or spiritual and devotional experiences to be *the* foundation for a Christian's walk with Christ; instead, the issue is trust in God—not feelings. Wesley did nonetheless hold that believers can have subjective experiences in Christ that cause growth in the assurance of their salvation, even though words strain to describe those experiences. He once wrote that Christians can have an internal testimony of the Spirit, "an inward impression of the soul, whereby the Spirit of God immediately and directly witnesses to my spirit that I am a child of God, that Jesus Christ hath loved me . . . that all my sins are blotted out, and I, even I, am reconciled to God."[34]

This assurance and testing would be discerned via the fruit of the Spirit: "love, joy, peace, patience, kindness, goodness, faithfulness, gentleness, self-control," (Gal. 5:22–23). Persons, in Wesleyan tradition, who claim Christian identity but who do not exhibit fruit of the Spirit will eventually have their faith confession questioned. The fruits of the Spirit were important for gauging one's assurance of the Spirit's presence; but growth in holy living was also critical to Wesley on sanctification and assurance. For example, Wesley saw keeping a clear conscience and keeping the Bible's commandments as characteristic of those in Christ. Again, Wesley believed Christianity was a lifestyle, something that informs and transforms daily living, and not merely a body of doctrines separate from spiritual practice or lived devotion.

Most famously, Wesley believed that sanctification was not only gradual but also instantaneous. (For contrast's sake, the Reformed tradition teaches sanctification as a lifelong, gradual process.) Wesley's twofold, and seemingly contradictory, position has found many scholars spilling a great deal of ink in attempts to explain the view. He believed that whereas the Holy Spirit gradually draws the believer with grace to regeneration, culminating in a critical moment called salvation, so also the Spirit purges the believer's heart with sanctifying grace until there is a critical moment—a highly emotional and transformative moment—when the believer is entirely sanctified. (Later scholars have referred to these moments as crisis experiences.) Wesley believed instantaneous entire sanctification could happen, but that its occurrences were rare; he said he only knew a few Christians who were entirely sanctified.

Finally, Wesley believed in the Holy Spirit's continuing to do miraculous work. Throughout his own journal, Wesley recorded at least 240 cases of divine healing and one instance of deliverance (for two women tormented by the devil). He also witnessed believers, under his own ministry, speaking in tongues (*glossalalia*).[35] This understanding of the active workings of the Spirit accords with his conviction that Christianity is a lived experience.

ABIDING INFLUENCE

Wesley's desire to cure souls, his practical divinity, brought eminent results. In the United States he started the Methodist Church (even though he himself remained an Anglican to the end). His teachings about inner transformation, sanctification, and holy love captured the imagination of American pioneers, with the result that some one hundred years after his death, at the nineteenth century's end, the Methodist Church was noted as the largest Protestant denomination in the United States. His emphasis on the Holy Spirit laid the groundwork for later Pentecostal readings of the Bible and beliefs about the Spirit's work.

Despite his eventual enormous societal influence, some theologians have accused Wesley of Pelagianism.[36] But whereas Pelagius held that sinners could of their own volition both call on the mercy and grace of God and participate in their own salvation, Wesley adamantly affirmed that God is always the first mover. Specifically, by emphasizing prevenient grace, Wesley uniquely described the work of the Spirit in preparing a person's heart so that, equipped by grace, one could in turn respond to God and believe. This understanding of the Holy Spirit's activities in daily life would be appropriated and later modified by Methodists and Holiness (see Glossary) adherents.

Wesley's abiding influence leans less specifically on his teachings about the Holy Spirit and more toward his broader ministerial focus: the transformation of the whole human person. Others—in the monastic tradition particularly—also wrote about inner and mystical transformation, but situated within Roman Catholicism, they were often neglected or marginalized by nineteenth- and twentieth-century Western Christians. Wesley, by helping believers to esteem holiness and sanctification on the American frontier, served as an important historical gateway for Christianity's character in the United States today. That Christianity should involve a change of heart, that there are certain moral standards for Christians to follow, and that there are methods for pursuing God and his holy love—these all cohere together in a mixture that currently and significantly characterizes American Christianity.

While Wesley's faith and teachings were oriented around standard Christian categories—salvation, sanctification, holiness, the Church, and sacraments—he very much believed in the Bible as the authoritative rule for Christian life and thought. Others in Wesley's era would challenge not only those categories but the Bible's authority as well. Philosophical admixtures were exploding on the European continent that would make huge inroads into the practice and teaching of theology. Our next theologian, Friedrich Schleiermacher, proposed such new categories that sent shock waves rumbling, waves that continue to move right into our own era.

4
Friedrich Schleiermacher
(1768–1834)

HISTORICAL CONTEXT

*T*HE PHILOSOPHICAL TRICKLE that began in the Renaissance became a rushing torrent by the late eighteenth century. Questions in the Renaissance, raised by churchmen themselves but which posed no immediate threat to the existence of the biblical God, naturally and imperceptibly led to other questions that seemingly began to erode the foundations of this fundamental belief. Tides of the fourteenth- and fifteenth-century Renaissance were pushed in part by a revisitation of Aristotle's writings (384–322 BC). Aristotle's philosophical method was *from below*: he believed that what is true can be found in particular instances (e.g., physical matter, data, and observable phenomena) that point toward the ultimate essences of reality.

As the centuries flowed forward Western philosophers also investigated Plato's teaching (ca. 427–347 BC) that the universe is rooted in eternal ideas. Plato's philosophical method was one *from above*: he sought to determine the ideas and ideals of ultimate metaphysical reality and then ask how those extend themselves into physical reality. Neither of these two Greek philosophers believed in the personal God who is worshiped in the Judeo-Christian tradition, but they did propose fascinating and sophisticated ways to navigate reality. Aristotle and Plato's philosophical frameworks powerfully influenced Christian theological formulation,[37] and Aristotle's philosophy particularly helped spur scientific investigation as we know it today.

Some three hundred years after the Reformation—in Schleiermacher's era—the philosophical questions of the Renaissance were leading to further questions. Answers to those questions gradually challenged a traditional biblical understanding of reality. For example, if the earth was not the center of the universe—and Christians had long supposed, from their reading of Genesis, that it was—then what was the center? Nothing? For minds cultivated in Christianity, that was preposterous. A related question ensued: is the human race the universe's reason for being? Traditional Christian biblical interpretation had assumed for centuries that God created the whole universe precisely for the existence of humanity. In Schleiermacher's day, new scientific discoveries, and their secular philosophical interpretations, were seemingly answering these questions, which were first raised in the Renaissance, in ways that undermined the old European Christian worldview.

These new philosophical and scientific questions and discussions were exploding in Western Europe when Friedrich Schleiermacher came on the scene. Many Christians were unaware of the cataclysmic worldview shifts occurring around them. Though some, aware of these changes, demonized them as ill-intended or godless speculations and heresies, other Christians, particularly those in university roles or those in aristocratic classes, sought to engage in these philosophical and scientific discussions. Friedrich Schleiermacher walked on the intellectual scene amid this explosive philosophical matrix.

Born into the Reformed tradition, young Schleiermacher was deeply influenced by Moravian Pietists (the same tradition that profoundly influenced John Wesley). Then, after time in university studies, Schleiermacher experienced a crisis of faith. In a letter to his father he confessed he no longer believed that Jesus was God eternal or that Jesus' death atoned for human sin. Given the centrality of those two doctrines to Christianity, Schleiermacher surprisingly didn't completely abandon Christianity. Instead, and why he is renown today as an epic theologian, he worked diligently to integrate Christianity with his era's secular philosophy. Many thus call Schleiermacher the "father of liberal theology."

Much of post-Reformation Protestant theology was rational, not experiential and definitely not mystical. Protestant theologians during the first 250 years following the Reformation developed their theology in ways that appealed to people of reason, people who wanted substantial and sensible foundations for their beliefs and straightforward "this is what the Bible says" lines of argumentation. By Schleiermacher's time this theology had become experientially arid. Protestant theologians articulated Christian truth, but increasingly Western Europeans found this truth mechanical: truth was logical and understandable, but it lacked élan. Moreover, Protestant theology was overly constrained to the churches and their narrowly defined concerns.

These arid winds blew so long they caused a volatile reaction: romanticism, a philosophical movement characterized by feeling.

If one might pigeonhole Schleiermacher (admittedly difficult, as this prolific writer's work is so philosophically complex), we'd label him a romanticist. He wanted to *feel* Christianity rather than just intellectually understand it; he wanted to *experience* the truth of Christianity. Truth, if authentic, should manifest in life, Schleiermacher held, and not just be intellectually tenable. More particularly, for him as a professor, he wanted to articulate why Christianity was true at the personal level. In a book focusing on the doctrine of the Holy Spirit, it will be helpful for us to understand Schleiermacher's overarching concern permeating his views on several theological points and so discern his understanding of the Holy Spirit.

Though the romanticists were reacting to the dry rationalism of their philosophical predecessors, they nevertheless believed in the methodological fashion of the day: that understandings of truth and reality needed to be grounded in a dependable foundation. Consistently, romanticists sought to ground reality in human feeling. René Descartes (1596–1650) had said, "I think, therefore I am." For him, this proved an unassailable starting place for processing reality and moving toward truth, a rationalist position. Schleiermacher, following the lead of German idealist philosophers, subjectivized, or perhaps better, psychologized, Descartes' position and said, "I feel absolutely dependent, therefore I am." Even more, Schleiermacher believed that the feeling of absolute dependency not only proved that the human self exists but also that the universe and God exist.

Like a good romanticist and a good idealist, Schleiermacher believed the universe and everything in it is ultimately one, ultimately united in reason (an invisible but causative force). Human beings are particular instances, or manifestations, of the reason that permeates the universe (Plato averred similarly). That we feel dependent on people and things (e.g., water, food, life's necessities) outside ourselves, for instance, stems from our very nature as members of the universe. Our individual needfulness illustrates our identity as beings united to the vast universe. Describing our relation to life, God, and the universe, Schleiermacher once wrote, "Religion is the outcome neither of the fear of death, nor of the fear of God. It answers a deep need in man. It is neither a metaphysic, nor a morality, but above all and essentially an intuition and a feeling."[38] Seeing human beings as fundamentally religious and intuitive in character for Schleiermacher was self-evident. Yet some two hundred years after Schleiermacher, philosophers now know this is itself a very tentative perspective, one impossible to prove with science.[39]

For Schleiermacher it follows that Jesus was unique because he had a fully developed sense of dependency on God. According to Schleiermacher, Jesus did not have a divine nature, he was not supernatural, and he was not fundamentally different from any other human being. Rather, Jesus was unhindered in his awareness of, his visceral feeling regarding, God's presence. What was supernatural, what was God's gift to Jesus (and indirectly to the human race), was Jesus' own sense of utter God-dependency. Again, fundamental to human nature, for Schleiermacher, is consciousness of God.

By portraying Jesus in this light, Schleiermacher believed he both safeguarded the historical reality of Jesus and established a link to common humanity: Jesus' God-consciousness is possible for all people. We can have basically the same experience of God that Jesus did. It did not disturb Schleiermacher that he developed his philosophy at the expense of the biblical portrayal of Jesus.[40] This is critical: Schleiermacher believed human beings can, apart from God's revelation, know God. He *relocated the means of knowing God away from God's self-revelation and to human nature.* This shift eventually caused enormous tremors in the theological and philosophical arenas, and many theologians after Schleiermacher continually toil to shift the understanding back to God's self-revelation.

Why this long foray into Schleiermacher's larger philosophy? Simply, what liberties he took with the biblical text and with Jesus of Nazareth he took with the doctrines of salvation and the Holy Spirit. Straining those doctrines through a historical-philosophical sieve allowed Schleiermacher to align his beliefs with his preexisting commitments about reality and religion. Commenting on Schleiermacher, Albert Schweitzer once said that Schleiermacher did not "seek the Jesus of history but the Jesus Christ" of his own construction of Christianity. "The empirical reality [of Jesus of Nazareth] simply does not exist for" Schleiermacher.[41]

THE HOLY SPIRIT

Committed to a naturalistic interpretation of reality and religion, Schleiermacher believed that the Holy Spirit works as the common spirit in Christian society. More precisely, when Jesus sent the Holy Spirit to his disciples, he was sending them a common mentality, a common attitude, a common disposition toward one another, God, and life. What Jesus had experienced in his unencumbered God-consciousness was now theirs as a community, albeit in less perfect form. For Schleiermacher the Spirit is not the third member of the transcendent triune God but *an impulse* within the Christian communion, assembling together, disciplining one another, baptizing new converts into a shared God-consciousness, working together, and evangelizing the world.

The Spirit is not something external that breaks into our reality, if by external we mean something beyond our human nature. Instead, when a person believes in Jesus Christ he or she begins to share the same experience, the same perception of reality, as the Christian community. For Schleiermacher, to become Christ's disciple, then, is to begin to move into the God-consciousness that belonged to Jesus, who initially passed this to his apostles, and that subsequent Christians in turn share with others. One day, Schleiermacher believed, the whole world will thus be Christianized.

ABIDING INFLUENCE

While we have explored a substantial amount about Schleiermacher in order to see precious little about the Holy Spirit, he nevertheless represents a significant historic precedent. Across the theological spectrum and consistently through Schleiermacher's interpretation of the Bible, he enabled philosophy to trump biblical revelation.[42] Schleiermacher did this in good faith. He was in no way attempting to undermine the Christian framework. He was not a religious pluralist believing that all paths lead to the same mountaintop called God. He never attempted to deconstruct the biblical text. Instead, at his genius-level best he buttressed the faith with a sophisticated overlay that made sense to him and many others within his historical context.

Schleiermacher sought to rebuild Christianity *from below*, starting with humanity and working up to God's existence. Particularly, Schleiermacher's Christianity focused on immanence—God is in and through all things—rather than transcendence—God is beyond all things, beyond all existence save his own. Later critics would begin to see pantheistic—God is all, all is God—tendencies in Schleiermacher's version of Christianity. Schleiermacher, however, would not be the last to move in this direction.

Like Wesley, the Anabaptists, and the Pietists before him, Schleiermacher made experience central to Christianity; many scholars deem this his crucial and positive theological contribution. Maintaining apostolic teaching is critical, but Christianity is more than a body of ideas (though beliefs and ideas shape and lead to the experiential elements). With this understanding of religion, Schleiermacher worked diligently to present and defend the notion that Christianity produces existential results and that it makes a difference in daily life. Millions of Protestants whose ministers were trained in seminaries owe something of their experiential understanding of Christianity to Schleiermacher.

Yet not all Protestants, or Protestant theologians, embraced Schleiermacher's philosophical shifts and romanticism's influence in Europe. Many Protestant believers were simply ignorant of the philosophical developments inside the universities around them and so were blind to their implications for Christian life and faith. In contrast, Abraham Kuyper, a late-nineteenth-early-twentieth-century leader in the Reformed tradition, was aware of and resistant to these dramatic philosophical shifts. Kuyper's nuanced teachings about the Holy Spirit are examined next.

5
Abraham Kuyper
(1837–1920)

HISTORICAL CONTEXT

*T*heologians differently influence the Church and theology. Some do so via their teaching; direct mentoring of future leaders pays dividends. Other theologians influence Christendom through their publications, dispersing their ideas and innovations through the print medium and characterizing entire traditions. A select few other theologians shape theology and belief in their own day primarily through their celebrity. Of the latter was Abraham Kuyper.

Known by today's historians and theologians as much for his theory of knowledge[43] and his momentous engagement with society as for his theology, Kuyper was a widely influential Dutch Reformed leader in the Netherlands. After his university education, and after several years as a pastor, a professor, and a member of the Dutch parliament, Kuyper served as Prime Minister of the Netherlands from 1901 to 1905. He remained interested in education throughout his life and was a champion of private education in Dutch policy formation even after his stint as Prime Minister. Late into life he taught theology and lectured in universities.

Nineteenth-century European universities had surging sway on society. Perceiving secular philosophies waxing in the universities, some Christian leaders opposed them in their sermons, school lessons, and publications. Commitments to God and godly values were also, many Protestants believed, perceptibly being sidelined by secular philosophies operative in governmental policies and decisions. Kuyper was among those who believed that secular philosophy was not only contrary to Scripture but injurious to society because it was not grounded in Christian principles. Rather than retreat into his own Christian subculture, however, Kuyper sought through persuasion and politics to integrate Reformed Christian beliefs into the larger society. Kuyper promoted a Christian societal vision, one he believed could compete with the growing vision of "modernism" (or secularism). He believed Christian beliefs and values should permeate government and society so that Christianity's outcomes would attract people over secular attempts to shape government and society. Important to his societal policy, he promoted the separation of church and state, a position brought to the United States and instilled by Reformed European immigrants.

Theologically, the Reformed tradition greatly emphasizes God's sovereignty (absolute rule). Typifying this, Kuyper said, "Violating nothing, God adapts Himself to the delicate and manifold needs of man's spiritual being; and reveals His divine omnipotence in the victory over the endless and gigantic obstacles which nature puts in His way."[44] Most Christians would immediately recognize Reformed theology, Calvinism as it is sometimes called,[45] in light of its special commitment to the doctrine of predestination, summarized as follows: God, in a decree from eternity, chose who will be saved; God's will is never thwarted or frustrated; and God is in absolute control. Kuyper asserted, "No creature can exclude itself from the divine control."[46] We cannot know, say the Reformed, why God elected some for salvation and not others; this means that salvation is solely God's gift and owes nothing to human work. Some Reformed theologians hold to double predestination, the doctrine that God has chosen not only who will be saved but also who will be damned. Kuyper, who did not espouse double predestination, believed the Holy Spirit comes to enact and complete God's plan of predestination.

THE HOLY SPIRIT

In order to understand Kuyper's view of the Spirit, let's examine his belief in the Spirit's role in election. Again, God planned even before creation to choose some—the elect—for salvation. Kuyper believed the Spirit, at imperceptible moments, encounters an elect person and implants a new life principle. For instance, John the Baptist received the Spirit's new life principle while in his mother's womb, said Kuyper.[47] Jesus said that, like the wind's mysterious movement, the Spirit moves mysteriously without our understanding (Jn. 3:8); so it is, Kuyper reasoned, with those who are given the new life principle. The elect person does nothing to prepare for or receive the Spirit's regenerative

gift; it is solely God's act. This is central for Kuyper's understanding of the Spirit and God's sovereignty. Before this indiscernible
moment, the elect one is dead in sin, but after this moment she
or he is *capable* of faith. When actual belief occurs is not know-
able, yet because of the Spirit's sovereign work one is given a
faith capacity, something Kuyper called regeneration. Many
theologians locate the process of regeneration *after* the person
comes to conscious faith.

So the Holy Spirit gives the faith capacity, but there is
more. The Spirit also *preserves* the faith capacity—the gift of
regeneration—in and for the elect person no matter whether
the elect is spiritually "asleep" or living in sin. The faith capacity,
then, can be dormant within the person; again, the gift and its
preservation are solely God's acts and do not depend on the
person. Eventually, Kuyper held, the spiritually sleeping and/
or sinning person will be called by God in two ways: inward
and outward.

The *outward* call is the word of God; churches perform this
through preaching and the sacraments: God thus involves
churches in the regenerative process. With the *inward* call the
Holy Spirit works internally in the elect, an action whereby,
Kuyper said, "the Lord our God enters human consciousness
to communicate His thoughts, clothed in human thoughts and
speech."[48] There are then two harmonizing elements, external-
objective (outward) and internal-subjective (inward), to God's
call and purpose. Harkening to Martin Luther's theological
pattern, Kuyper believed that word and Spirit energize the
faith capacity so that the formerly dormant elect person's faith
is awakened. As with most Protestants, Kuyper viewed faith

itself as a gift of the Holy Spirit; in Ephesians 2:8 Saint Paul says, "For by grace you have been saved through faith; and that not of yourselves, it is the gift of God."

God's call, Kuyper further specified, convicts of sin and justifies the elect person. When a person realizes guilt for sin and yearns for salvation, Kuyper held that the Spirit is working inwardly; so too with an internal sense of one's justification by God. Conviction and justification are two sides of one coin for Kuyper: faith both reproves sin and justifies in Christ Jesus. That's not all, Kuyper believed, because conversion too is the Spirit's internal engagement. Conversion is the elect person's interior awareness of new life—the resurrection power of Jesus. For the first time, one enjoys mystical union with Christ amid conversion. Before conversion the elect one was passive to the Spirit's operations; after conversion the elect person responds to the Spirit and is aware of death to the sinful self. The Spirit thus accomplishes God's sovereignly decreed work.

As beautiful as conversion is, it is not the goal, per Kuyper. God desires greater: sanctification. Sanctification makes believers' natures holy. The elect are neither more forgiven nor more justified by sanctification; truly, God forgives us through Christ, and Christ's atonement reckons us holy. But sanctification progressively removes sin's internal stain and makes Christ's righteousness tightly inhere. Kuyper believed that the elect experience existential transformation via sanctification; one's whole self is involved. To wit, sanctification evokes holy dispositions (and holy dispositions enable good works) in believers' hearts, and believers' wills are softened to become more Christlike. In sanctification God's Spirit fills our hearts with love and empowers control over passions. According to Kuyper, most nonredeemed people are enslaved to their passions, which wildly drive sinners in helter-skelter directions, "but the passions of the saint are controlled in a different way. Sanctification gives them another direction. He feels their whip and spur, but they are to him the violence of a foreign power. Wherefore St. Paul declares, 'It is no more I that do it, but sin that dwelleth in me.' And no passion can overtake him which in the power of God he cannot master and control."[49]

Did Kuyper believe entire sanctification was possible in life? There were contemporaries who espoused so: Methodists and Holiness (see Glossary) Christians. Divergently, Kuyper believed it prideful to assert sinlessness: the old, sinful, Adamic nature eradicated before death. The Holy Spirit certainly aims to mortify the sinful nature, but, disagreeing with Wesley on this matter, Kuyper believed total sanctification impossible short of death.

God's Spirit redeems the elect, averred Kuyper, but the Spirit also effects creation; Kuyper's position here has been foundational for subsequent theologians. He believed the Holy Spirit, long confessed by historic Christians as Lord and life-giver (*creator spiritus*), completes and perfects creation. In fact, the elect's salvation and transformation are, for Kuyper, a single element of God's eschatological—end of history—goal. Kuyper spoke about this universal quality: "The work of the Holy Spirit consists in leading all creation *to its destiny*, the final purpose of which is the glory of God."[50] In time's beginning the Spirit hovered over creation's surface (Gen. 1:2). He will faithfully guide creation to its end, something Kuyper called the new beginning. Kuyper thus introduced a cosmic element to the Spirit's work. God's Spirit yearns for transformation for the elect *and* God's good creation.

The most unique element of Kuyper's theology, particularly from a Reformed perspective emphasizing human nature's total depravity, was his teaching on common grace, a dynamic innovation. How do we account for any good sinners do? Why is there a moral quality to all human cultures? Why is it that non-Christians exhibit amazing talents? These questions require a thoughtful response in interfacing the Christian worldview with society in general. Particularly, Kuyper wondered, how should Christians interface with nonbelievers for the sake of goodness and justice? To resolve these issues Kuyper proposed common grace.

Like Luther and others, Kuyper maintained the doctrine of total depravity: there is neither righteousness nor impulse toward righteousness in fallen humanity. Left to itself human nature would therefore run headlong into wickedness and destruction. God, through his Spirit, and because he loves his creation, bestows on sinners a measure of grace that restrains this tendency toward evil. Sin and evil are therefore negated to some extent. What emerges is a measure of grace that works positively, enabling unredeemed people to do good and to benefit God's creation. As some people are outstanding statesmen, others are gifted artisans, lawyers, or military geniuses—these gifts rise from the grace of the Spirit. (How this occurs Kuyper did not clarify; in fact, he qualified he had no biblical precedent to so argue, saying the Scriptures only show God's Spirit giving gifts to the elect.)[51] Because this grace is not special saving grace bestowed on the elect, according to Kuyper, it should more accurately be called common grace. In this view, Kuyper saw Christians working alongside nonbelievers for the common good because of God's grace.[52] However, Kuyper did not believe common grace was part of the Spirit's work of salvation. He strongly argued that those who said "the Lord had His elect, even tho [sic] they never heard of the Scripture," bordered on pantheism—that God is all and all is God, a belief challenging apostolic teaching about hearing the gospel for both faith and salvation.[53] Nevertheless, in Kuyper's day, increasingly more churchmen argued that people in other religions could be saved apart from hearing the word of God.

Finally, Kuyper kept other important points. He taught that the Holy Spirit formed and forms the Church as foundational to God's eternal plan. The Spirit illumines God's word and makes it alive within individual believer's hearts. At the communal level, Kuyper asserted, the Spirit guides the Church in her own self-governance, especially when she seeks God in prayer. Kuyper also held that the Spirit's charismatic gifts, operating throughout Christian history, were still active. The Holy Spirit is wonderfully active across the spectrum of Christian life.

ABIDING INFLUENCE

Kuyper is renowned for constructing a vision of Christianity characterized by both salt and light, a Christian interaction with society offering an alternative to secularism's growing tide. Since his time the Reformed have followed Kuyper's cues and have similarly sought to empower the whole Church to engage issues like caring for the poor, understanding the appropriate role of governmental structures, establishing a just fiscal economy, and developing Christian ethics.

In his doctrine of the Holy Spirit, Kuyper typifies the general Protestant tendency to unite the word and the Spirit in the work of salvation; God accomplishes salvation through the harmonious enterprise of Spirit and word. God's word (revelation) doesn't work alone to save. Non-Protestant Christians and non-Christians may well wonder why Protestants place such an emphasis on the Bible, preaching, and the Spirit's saving work therein. Historically, the answer is because influential leaders like Kuyper, using positions of societal prominence and teaching their theology for decades, have further ensconced the word-Spirit tandem in the collective Protestant consciousness. Regarding salvation, the Reformed today are committed to God's word as coworking with the Holy Spirit. Influenced by the Reformed tradition, the great bulk of the world's Pentecostals, commonly stereotyped as overemphasizing the Spirit's role, consistently maintain that God uses his word and Spirit together.

Friedrich Schleiermacher's notion of God-consciousness opened vistas for the possibility of non-Christians' knowing God. Committed to orthodox Christian tradition, Kuyper also established a theory about the nonelect in ways including them in God's purposes. With common grace, the concept that God gives gifts to the nonredeemed for the sake of society's common good and creation's flourishing, Kuyper opened subtle avenues of theological speculation for how non-Christians may be involved in God's actions. Creation and salvation are distinct; the Spirit blesses creation and sinners with common grace, though that doesn't save sinners. Though the Holy Spirit is the Lord and life-giver, that fact does not equate to spiritual salvation in Kuyper's theology.

Kuyper's doctrine of common grace evinced a more nuanced understanding of God's own activities in human life than did Schleiermacher, who rooted religion and religious deeds in the human feeling of absolute dependency. Is it true that God's Spirit exclusively works through Christians? During Kuyper's time many answered no, but many others posed answers bordering on pantheism. The categories of God and creation were gradually being blurred. One theologian who intentionally sought to reestablish distinct boundaries between God and creation was Karl Barth, the wildly influential theologian who we'll meet in our next chapter.

6
Karl Barth
(1886–1968)

HISTORICAL CONTEXT

*T*HEOLOGIANS RARELY make an immediate impact on the daily life and faith of Christians. True, they teach their own students, who in turn might go and teach their teachers' doctrine in a local church parish. But most theologians who have shaped the character of Protestantism did so only after their own deaths. Theology has to be written, disseminated, processed, and received by others; all of that requires time. Frequently, decades after a theologian's era, the nuance and flavor of a theologian's interpretive framework deeply sink their roots into the Christian character as pastors preach a theologian's system. For example, though mostly unaware of it, millions of Protestants (and Roman Catholics) think about God and process their private lives like good Augustinians.[54] Most of us read our Bibles without any awareness that we are doing so following the interpretive leads and insights of prominent theologians. Our reality as Christians we owe staggeringly to those who preceded us. As Bernard of Chartres (d. AD 1124) once said, "We stand on the shoulders of giants."

Today, millions of Protestants follow Christ in the glow of Karl Barth's theological commitments. Early twentieth-century theological liberalism won over vast swaths of Protestant leaders and laypersons in Europe and the United States. Amid this context, Barth brought a theological and moral courage. Most prominently he was the chief author of the Barmen Declaration, a letter he signed with other German church leaders, including Dietrich Bonhoeffer, who together challenged the accumulating authority of Hitler and the Nazis in 1934. (The Nazis brutalized vocal opponents, so for safety's sake Barth left Germany.) Standing up to Hitler was followed by a lifetime of battling both liberals and conservatives over theological matters. And truly, very few on either side of the theological spectrum initially embraced his ideas. (Even today he is a divisive figure, even if influential.)

Liberals thought Barth's theology was glaringly *from above*; he believed we truly can know God's revelation, and so he proceeded to develop his entire theological system in light of God's self-revelation. Liberals tend to believe this is arrogant, overreaching, and an unnecessarily exclusive view of other religions. Conservatives, on the other hand, were wary that Barth's system was permeated with philosophical terminology not always committed to historic Christian vocabulary. Ironically, Barth openly voiced his own disdain for a liberal theology overly committed to philosophy. He thought Schleiermacher's "God-consciousness" as a starting place for theological development was preposterous both because it caused salvation to be effected by human works and because it was a fundamental misunderstanding of human nature; there is nothing by ourselves we sinners can do to know God.

Despite the controversies he provoked, Barth is a theological giant. Consistent with his Reformed background he believed God freely and sovereignly revealed himself in history to sinners. Specifically, and here Barth agreed with Martin Luther, God revealed himself in and through Jesus Christ. All of salvation history (see Glossary) was expressly planned by God for the coming of Jesus—and Jesus' incarnation was God-ordained whether or not the Fall occurred. The preeminent revelatory word is neither the Bible nor preaching, though Barth believed that God's word comes via both. Preeminence singularly belongs to God incarnate, Jesus of Nazareth. (This emphasis has seen Barth's theology variously labeled as Word-centered and/or Christocentric.) Because Jesus-as-God's-revelation is history's center and apex,[55] and because Jesus' work and identity beg reflection on his relationship to the Father and the Holy Spirit, Barth established the Trinity as his theological system's foundation.[56] A global flourish of study, writing, teaching, and spirituality about the triune God has followed in Barth's wake in mid-to-late-twentieth- and even twenty-first-century Christendom.

THE HOLY SPIRIT

Holding Christ as God's preeminent revelation and placing his theological emphasis on the triune God's self-revelation, Barth permeated his writings with reflections on the Spirit's person and work. In history God was enfleshed as Jesus. Barth, interpreting the Gospel birth narratives, reasoned that the Spirit was the causative agent in Jesus' conception. Put differently, the Virgin Mary, herself a sinner, was not the incarnation's focal point so much as the Holy Spirit (a clear critique of Roman Catholic Mariology); Mary received the Spirit's work but did not contribute to it. For Barth, true to his sweeping Trinitarian commitments, this means it was the Holy Spirit who made Jesus the God-man. Jesus owed his identity—his person and his work—to the Spirit.

Jesus entered history and accomplished our salvation. Barth called this the objective revelation of God. For our salvation's sake, it is insufficient that Jesus accomplished the atonement in the past. Atonement needs to be appropriated, or actualized, in someone's life—now—for it to matter personally. This, Barth believed, is why the Holy Spirit advances today. God's Spirit brings Christ's redemptive power to us and unites us with Christ. How that unification precisely happens, Barth said, is a mystery; here he reflects his Reformed heritage. He did assert, however, that the biblical teaching on salvation requires a human response; redemption does not merely *happen to* a sinner; it needs the sinner's involvement. Again in keeping with a Reformed framework, salvation is entirely the work of God, but the sinner nevertheless, as Scripture teaches, must respond.

Barth thus affirmed the doctrine of total depravity but etched it with his own nuance. People are doomed as sinners, Barth believed, in the sense that "human nature has no capacity for revelation, no inherent ability to receive the Word of God. Any capacity is a graced one."[57] The Spirit gives that grace, but in redemption God's Spirit neither overwhelms nor overrules human nature. Truly, Barth averred, the Holy Spirit frees us to respond to God's salvific power. And faith, always the Spirit's generous gift, enables us to love. Human love, *eros* in Greek, is always self-serving and self-motivated, but God's love, *agape*, is self-giving and outwardly directed. *Agape*, born of the Spirit, instills both dignity and power within people. *Agape* turns us toward God. In salvation's existential actualization and appropriation, Barth taught that the Spirit is central. As with Wesley and Luther, Barth held that God is always the first mover—he moves with grace, faith, and love—and this is necessary because sinners are depraved and unrighteous.

According to Barth, salvation, objectively accomplished by Jesus and appropriated to us by the Spirit, is God's greatest miracle. It is a stunning miracle, and Barth refused to mundanely categorize it as self-actualization, as popular psychology today might define it, or as the enhancement of a person's religious or moral impulses, as Schleiermacher construed it. Salvation is something God effected, *without our help*, in history. Salvation began with Jesus Christ's story, a story of life and a freedom that is ours through the Spirit. Barth described salvation, being awakened to faith in Christ, with the metaphor of Spirit baptism: an immersion in God's Spirit.[58]

Spirit baptism had a connotation that predated Barth. Earlier in the twentieth century, particularly in the United States, Pentecostals had described experiences of the Spirit accompanied by speaking in tongues as baptism with the Holy Ghost, or simply Spirit baptism. In his theology, Barth expanded the meaning of Spirit baptism to include not just a specific moment but the Spirit's sweeping work in a person's life. For him Spirit baptism was a biblical metaphor that was all-inclusive of life in Christ.[59] Jesus' own story was Barth's basis for this expansive shift. Jesus' entire life was guided by and immersed (i.e., baptized) in the Spirit; Jesus' incarnation, ministry, death, and resurrection were all accomplished in the Spirit. The believer's story should follow Jesus' own story and thus be guided by the Spirit in the same way. In other words, Christian lives ought to be characterized similarly to Jesus' life.

Theologians often bring clarity to our vision. Barth's understanding of the Christian life as Spirit baptism produces a beautiful perspective on life in Christ. The sixteenth-century Reformers were adamant that God *counts* or *reckons* us righteous in Christ (Rom. 4); believers remain sinners, but God views us through Christ's righteousness. Barth's theology pushes beyond mere reckoned righteousness. Spirit baptism, a life's reorientation for Barth, is a radical shift that transitions a person out of darkness into the domain of light. This change happens not merely in God's perspective; Barth insisted that Spirit baptism causes genuine inner transformation in a person's own character and personality. The person becomes a qualitatively new person. Describing the Christian experience, Barth called those undergoing Spirit baptism "disturbed sinners": while believers remain sinners, the experience is that sin is no longer allowed to rule. The Spirit disturbs and disrupts former patterns of sin.[60]

Additionally unique to Barth was his belief that the Spirit awakens a calling, a sense of mission, in the believer's life. Millions of global Charismatics (see Glossary) today focus on the many different gifts that the Holy Spirit bestows. While Barth did not speak against the reality of the charismatic gifts, he believed there was something more central to the Christian life: the gospel. Barth likened Jesus' death and resurrection to the bread of life, the foremost element of the gospel. So for Barth, charismatic gifts are like the cake of the gospel; they are nice delicacies but are not central to the gospel.[61]

The mission is the gospel itself, for Barth. For him the critical gift of the Spirit was that Christians be witnesses, those who proclaim the gospel of Jesus. Christians are Christ followers; they not only follow Jesus himself, Barth believed, they should follow Jesus' mission. God's Spirit drove Jesus *into* his ministry and then drove him *during* his ministry. The apostles worshiped Jesus, but they also performed Jesus' mission. They preached God's word—Jesus Christ and him crucified (1 Cor. 2:2). Similarly, averred Barth, all believers must be Spirit-driven to preach the gospel.

Barth believed the gospel was God's chosen means, God's most powerful means, to transform the whole creation. How are darkened hearts overcome? When the good news is shared. Indeed, Barth so promoted evangelism as the tool to transform the broken world that he vehemently opposed apologetics: using logic, reason, rhetorical arguments, persuasion, and natural philosophical evidences to try to win nonbelievers. (In philosophical terminology an apology is a defense.) Schleiermacher and other theological liberals had earlier made philosophical apologies. This aggravated Barth because he believed they had gravely truncated and compromised the Christ-given and apostolic message: the gospel. With this emphasis in Barth, we can see why so many Evangelicals (see Glossary) view him an important dialogue partner.

Barth further developed his theology of Christian mission:

- By himself Jesus defeated Satan, death, and sin. We add nothing to his victory and saving work. Barth is famous for emphasizing the anthem *Christus victor!* Christians should celebrate the glorious salvation Christ wrought.

- Mission defines the Church's very essence. Mission is *not* optional. Not all Christians should be professional missionaries, but all Christians should be living missional lives. Not only a theological commitment of Barth's, this mitigates against the pastor-laity dichotomy that produces apathy among lay people and overburdens clergy.

- People's conversion, not the propping up of any cultural vantage point or political platform, is the goal of missions. As Barth knew, too many post-Reformation Christian nations shamefully practiced colonialism.

- Mission for Christ is not an opportunity for imperialistic efforts on behalf of one's own culture. This means Christians should respect other religions while always recognizing that those are both failed and false.

- Because Christ seeks to transform the whole creation, and with it the entirety of human nature, missions should include alleviating people's physical and social plights. Enterprises like education, medical care, and humanitarian aid are important, but they should never become the main focus. Here it is helpful to remember that Barth once famously said sermons should be preached by pastors who have "the Bible in one hand and the daily newspaper in the other." (He said this amid his alarm over the rise to power of the Nazis—the church cannot be ignorant of her context.)

- The goal of missions work is building a missionary church. God's goal is that the whole human race be involved in his own mission and purpose. The Church, then, replicates herself in the doing of her mission.[62]

Characterizing Protestant theology on God's Spirit, Barth believed the Church is neither merely a human society nor a moralizing institution. The Church finds her identity in the Holy Spirit: collectively we are a temple for God's indwelling. Living in and for Christ, the Church exists through the Holy Spirit. This means the Christian community indwells *koinōnia*—fellowship—rooted in Christ and continually renewed by the Spirit. This Holy Spirit-ual quality then means the Church is both visible and invisible. It is obviously visible because it consists of members, polity, rituals, moral teachings, and the like. It is invisible because its life and unity draw on a divine source. Nonbelievers cannot know what this spiritual quality is like without being in Christ and his Spirit.

The Spirit creates and indwells the Church. The sovereign God, the Spirit, is in control, not ecclesiarchs or church members. The Spirit liberates believers, but not to the extent that we control the Spirit. Here Barth was clearly reacting to Roman Catholics and other sacramental Christians who he believed inextricably tethered the Spirit's work to the sacramental system. True, God graciously gave sacraments, but Barth did not believe the Spirit was imprisoned in them. The Spirit is the sovereign God. He answers to neither believers nor ecclesiastical officials. He is bound only to Christ and the Father.

ABIDING INFLUENCE

While his theological writings were permeated with reflections on the Spirit, Barth died before he ever wrote a book specifically about God's Spirit. Nevertheless, he remains renowned in the history of theology because he caused such a redirection of the whole theological enterprise, including his fresh appreciation for the Holy Spirit's work. His dogged commitment to the doctrines of revelation, election, and the Trinity challenged the mainstream liberal theological trend of his day; and through Barth's theological teachings a course of exploration was outlined for many others to develop.

For emphasizing Jesus Christ's significance, Barth is admired by all orthodox Christians. Some find his Christological positions exaggerated, carrying more weight than a careful scriptural study can bear. But because he put Christ at the center of his system, and indeed of all human history, Barth is esteemed if not universally accepted.

Barth's teaching that the Spirit impels evangelistic mission for both believers and the Church is certainly not original. Catholics and Orthodox were doing missions and being missional in different ways for nineteen centuries before Barth's era. Protestants too have a long and storied history of missionary endeavors, and Pentecostals at the turn of the twentieth century would send missionaries around the world for reasons fascinatingly similar to Barth's teachings. Still, Barth intentionally anchored mission to the person and work of the Holy Spirit. This vital insight has offered all Christians a way to better understand the nature of the Spirit and our own calling as Jesus' disciples.

Though in the twentieth century Barth celebrated the Spirit's presence and operation, he wasn't alone. Across the Atlantic, small Christian groups in the United States sought the Holy Spirit's presence and action in ways different than Barth had construed. These Christians were the Pentecostals. Our next chapter examines J. Rodman Williams, a theologian who, although himself a Charismatic, presented a very Pentecostal understanding of God's Spirit.

7
J. Rodman Williams
(1918–2008)

ODAY THERE ARE SOME two billion Christians in the world. Approximately one billion of those are Roman Catholics. Some six hundred million Christians are Pentecostals. The reader may be surprised to know that Pentecostals now outnumber all the other types of Protestants in the world combined.[63] This is particularly staggering given that Pentecostalism first began in 1901. Over one-fourth of Christendom traces its immediate roots to a date only some 110 years in the past. How do we account for this development? If we talk to Pentecostals, the answer will immediately point toward a profound postconversion experience of the Holy Spirit. In churches, home-hosted small groups, and prayer meetings the Spirit touches Christians in deep and profound ways.

Up through World War II Pentecostals were marginalized as "holy rollers," "enthusiasts," "yokels," "hicks," and "jumpers" by less-than-sympathetic Christians. Undeterred by those stereotypes, many Pentecostal preachers and evangelists traveled across the United States, holding revival meetings and telling of a life-transforming experience in the Spirit of God that parallels the day of Pentecost (Acts 2). In the 1950s several Pentecostals—William Branham, Gordon Lindsay, and Oral Roberts, most prominently—employed magazines, radio, and television to widely broadcast the news about the vibrant life and miraculous power at work in their ministries. These independent-minded Pentecostals made non-Pentecostals aware of the powerful dynamic of the Holy Spirit.

The Pentecostal movement's indelible marking of non-Pentecostal Christians was nationally noted in 1960, when both *Newsweek* and *Time* magazine ran articles[64] about Dennis Bennett, an Episcopalian priest in Van Nuys, California, who was filled with the Spirit and spoke in tongues. New things were astir, truly. Some Roman Catholics, hungry for spiritual renewal and encouraged that Vatican II supported the Spirit's freshly blowing winds, experienced similar phenomena in 1967, when students and faculty at Duquesne and Notre Dame encountered the Holy Spirit's power and spoke in tongues. Today the outbreak of spiritual gifts (charisms or *charismata* in biblical Greek) among non-Pentecostals is broadly known as the Charismatic movement.

Pentecostals are known for being vocal about their experiences; they say the Spirit precisely impels them *to share* about the Lord. Important for our study, however, is that prior to 1988 no Pentecostal theologian had written a decisively Pentecostal systematic theology. Sure, several Pentecostal theologians had written systematic studies (usually as training manuals for their own denominations), but none sought to incorporate and integrate either the Pentecostal experience or Pentecostal commitments in a thoroughgoing manner so that an entire body of theology was decidedly Pentecostalized. J. Rodman Williams's *Renewal Theology: Systematic Theology from a Charismatic Perspective*[65] is an attempt to do just that: bringing the profound experience of the Holy Spirit's infilling to bear on all theological categories.

Himself a Presbyterian, Williams was filled with God's Spirit in 1965. Holding a PhD in philosophy of religion and ethics, he was initially a pastor and then a professor, first at Melodyland School of Theology and then at Regent University School of Divinity. His second volume of *Renewal Theology*, titled *Salvation, the Holy Spirit, and Christian Living*, reads like an apology (defense) for the Charismatic experience. Apparently his goal was to give Charismatics themselves a biblical grounding. Clearly, he intended to deflect charges that the Charismatic movement was without apostolic precedent or altogether unbiblical.[66] Because of this monumental effort, he is a significant voice for our understanding of both the Pentecostal and Charismatic movements themselves and the basis for what still other theologians, aware of those movements, are writing about the Holy Spirit.

THE HOLY SPIRIT

More extensively than the theologians we have reviewed thus far, Williams carefully explored biblical stories and passages to establish who and what the Holy Spirit is. Again, he wanted to ensure a biblical foundation to his theological positions. In Williams's biblical interpretation, God's Spirit is not an esoteric force working in the universe nor simply the relationships enjoyed by believers. The Spirit is God himself, functioning in life to illuminate, energize, and empower God's people for his purposes.

Williams himself was filled with the Spirit, and that experience made him love his Reformed tradition even more rather than take him from it. This is a common testimony of those claiming Holy Spirit infilling; Roman Catholics say they love the Mass, Mary, the sacraments, and the pope more, not less, for having this profound experience in God. Something about the reality of God's thick presence lights hearts on fire for one's own Christian environment.[67] In his own case, Williams wanted readers to understand that he was simply being consistent with John Calvin himself, who had said about God that "the recognition of Him consists more in living experience than in vain and high-flown speculation."[68] Williams kept consistency with his Reformed background—emphasizing that Christ's work objectively accomplished our salvation in history, discussing an eternal call of God foundational for our salvation, and affirming predestination. On the latter, however, he qualified double predestination (that God determines both salvation for some and damnation for others), asserting that the language about predestination in Scripture is only regarding salvation, not damnation. As Kuyper and Barth had previously averred, Williams taught that the Holy Spirit makes the preached word of God subjectively real and powerful in a person's life.

Also consistent with the Reformed tradition, Williams held that faith is rooted in the combination of the W/word (i.e., Bible, preaching, and Jesus) and the Spirit. God is the bedrock

for faith: "It is not grounded in a human decision to believe."
"God's grace," Williams said, "is the source, and faith the human
instrument." "No one, therefore, can make himself believe. It is
not a matter of working up faith . . . it is not a human leap in the
dark." In this regard faith is not a decision based in human reasoning, but God's eternal plan now applied as the Spirit's work
in someone's life. Per Williams, God is the author and source of
salvation, not us. We cannot claim any credit. Still, God won't
save us without our consent or involvement.[69]

Williams considered water baptism important but not what
converts one from a sinner to a Christian. Forgiveness, he
wrote, is found in Christ not the water. Williams affirmed that
the water is involved in our receiving God's grace, though he
did not clarify why this is the case. He clarified that water
baptism publicly demonstrates one's reception of forgiveness;
water baptism marks one as a Christ follower. For Williams,
salvation's essential element is the Holy Spirit indwelling one's
heart. The Spirit, not rites or ceremonies, makes people new.
God's Spirit cleanses our hearts, renews our minds, and sets our
wills free.[70]

God has more for believers than salvation, Williams claimed.
The Holy Spirit also sanctifies believers by transforming them
into Christ's likeness, a transformation incorporating moral perfection. Jesus taught on sanctification; he said, "Be perfect" (Matt.
5:48). Jesus was accordingly prohibiting anger, lust, divorce,
false vows, and retaliation against one's enemies. Williams
asserted that sanctification is characterized by the absence of
sinful behavior: the Spirit indwells believers and immediately
challenges their flesh, their sinful selves. Sanctification is also

expressed by the presence of sacrificial love for one's enemies (Matt. 5:44). Negatively—via canceling sin—and positively—via growing in love—the sanctification process is lifelong.

God sanctifies us, but we are involved too. Williams said sanctification involves *"God all the way through man all the way."*[71] We must obey the Spirit's conviction of sin and his impelling us toward righteousness. True to the Reformed tradition, Williams clarified that though we share in the sanctification process, our security resides in the Lord, not ourselves. Williams realized some taught entire sanctification was possible in this life. Again true to his Reformed heritage, he disagreed.

Within his twentieth-century Charismatic context, it is noteworthy that Williams believed the Holy Spirit comes to fill people who are *already* believers. Williams reasoned that the disciples were Christians *before* the Holy Spirit came upon them in Jerusalem at Pentecost. Similarly, the Samaritans in Acts 8:14–17 believed before they received the Spirit's infilling; those of the centurion's household in Acts 10:44–46 were saved before the Spirit was poured out on them, and they spoke in tongues during Peter's ministry there; and the disciples in Ephesus were Christians (hence *disciples*) before Paul laid hands on them to receive the Holy Spirit and speak in tongues, according to Acts 19:1–7. Williams further made his case by similarly noting and interpreting several passages in the Epistles. Vital for his positions and teachings, Williams argued that Spirit baptism is both possible for, and to be expected in the life of, people who are already Christians.

Across Christendom's spectrum, theologians have debated the meaning and significance of these same biblical texts. And for centuries Protestants have typically argued that the Holy Spirit enters Christians' hearts through faith, particularly at conversion, while Roman Catholics and the Eastern Orthodox have long contended that the Spirit is present for the believer through water baptism—God's appointed means of grace. So their question for Williams would be: does the Spirit come *again*? Isn't his coming at Christian initiation (i.e., conversion and/or water baptism) sufficient? What is the import of a second coming of the Spirit?

Williams contended, in defense of the Charismatic experience, that God's Spirit comes to fill the believer after conversion. These post-initiation infillings of the Holy Spirit empower believers for the Church's mission. And just as the apostles saw the Spirit come repeatedly in the expansion and ministry of the Church, so contemporary believers might expect the Spirit's coming in their own lives. Williams believed the Spirit comes in this way because he read about it in the Bible and because he himself experienced "baptism in the Holy Spirit," an aptly descriptive phrase.[72] Just like water baptism in the ancient world soaked and drenched the new Christian, Williams believed that the contemporary believer subjectively becomes immersed, soaked and drenched in the Spirit.

While Williams did not speak firsthand about his own experience of Spirit baptism, he wrote that Spirit baptism "is a totality of penetration with the Holy Spirit whereby, in a new way, all areas of one's being—body, soul, and spirit (the conscious and the subconscious depths)—become sensitized to the divine presence and activity."[73] Further, he quoted the famous nineteenth-century revival preacher Charles G. Finney

(1792–1875), "the Holy Spirit descended upon me in a manner that seemed to go through me, body and soul. . . . Indeed it seemed to come in waves and waves of liquid love . . . like the very breath of God. . . it seemed to fan me like immense wings. . . . I wept aloud with joy and love; and I do not know but I should say I literally bellowed out the unutterable gushings of my heart."[74] Thousands of Pentecostal and Charismatic descriptions aver similarly, often with poetic meter and rhythm, to the affective and emotional dimensions of this experience.

Charismatics and Pentecostals regularly teach that Spirit baptism is accompanied by speaking in tongues (*glossolalia* in biblical Greek). Williams looked to Acts, where Luke describes five different occasions where God's Spirit descended on people (2:4; 8:17–19; 9:10–19; 10:45–46; 19:6). In Acts, speaking in tongues, Williams said, "was clear evidence that the Holy Spirit had been given. Speaking in tongues was *the* evidence in Jerusalem."[75]

As Williams developed his understanding, he noted diverse purposes for tongues. It is a way to give praise to God in the Holy Spirit. Just as music helps us to express our love for God in emotional ways, so also speaking in tongues is a kind of transcendent utterance offered to the Lord in joy. To carry this point Williams quoted Larry Tomczak, a Roman Catholic layman,

> I felt the rapturous and exultant joy of the Lord surging through me, and the more profuse my praise, the more intense became my desire to magnify the name of my Savior. I grew impatient with the inadequacy of the

English language to fully express all that I was feeling, how much I loved God. Then, just at the right moment, new words began to flow from my heart. . . . I could not restrain my tongue, and my lips began to stammer, as a new language hopped, skipped, and somersaulted from my mouth. The language was foreign to my ears, a heavenly language only God would understand. It was praise that had surged through my whole being to seek expression through the Holy Spirit in a new transcendence.[76]

Another purpose for tongues, Williams believed, was that it signifies God's doing something new in history, a partial fulfillment of Joel's prophecy (2:28–32) concerning the end of history. Williams developed another purpose: tongues are a form of nonrational prayer to God. This kind of prayer, he noted, allows believers, and/or the Spirit inside believers (Rom. 8:26–27), to pray with spiritual directness and immediacy. Amid speaking in tongues, the human voice speaks, but there is no divine compulsion forcing the human voice to mechanically sound. The believer, Williams reasoned, willingly speaks under the impulse of the Spirit. Looking at the Bible, Williams pointed out that, while Saint Paul preferred understandable praise and prayer, he did not therefore discount the unintelligible forms of those in tongues (1 Cor. 14:1–19).

ABIDING INFLUENCE

At the theological level Williams typifies the easily understandable nature of Pentecostalism. A Charismatic writing from the Reformed tradition, he interpreted biblical texts, unpacked their meaning, and suggested applications for today all in a way that nontheologians could understand. A similar simple approach has helped Pentecostalism explode in cultural contexts where people have little to no formal education. Pentecostals believe the Bible was written by the Holy Spirit for all people in all places and times. This interpretive approach has appealed to millions of people meeting God in ways consonant with the biblical characters.

Also very important for the Pentecostal and Charismatic movements is Williams's order of salvation (*ordo salutis* in Latin). That a person can be a believer before he or she is baptized with the Holy Spirit makes possible the experience for millions who are already Christian. This order is also formative for the teaching that there is God-given power available for Christian mission, evangelism, and living. Williams asserted that just as Jesus' ministry began with the Spirit's anointing him in the Jordan river, even though he was already the Son of God, so also believers can have a postinitiation experience of God that empowers them, changes them, and redirects their lives' paths.

Unsettling those of a rationalist bent, Williams and hundreds of millions of believers like him embrace emotion, gut-level dimensions of following Christ, and mystery. These qualities are critical in understanding why Pentecostals and Charismatics are numerically exploding around the world. Williams would point out that Jesus, Paul, and the apostles were not post-Enlightenment Europeans. Indeed, they were Middle Easterners who themselves witnessed miracles, demon exorcisms, and the invasion of God's Spirit into a world of darkness.

Pentecostalism, and in its wake the Charismatic movement, emphasizes a profoundly moving encounter with the Holy Spirit. In many respects this is a subjectivizing encounter, an encounter discussed in personal and private categories but that does not often take the larger creation into account. Late twentieth-century theologians, however, have prodded more deeply into global understandings of the Spirit's actions. One of those theologians is Jürgen Moltmann, the German theologian we will explore next.

8
Jürgen Moltmann
(1926–)

*W*e've seen throughout these pages that all theologians write in and for their own historical context. Indeed, we would agree that we are all shaped by our culture, our language, and our experiences. Jürgen Moltmann stands out among our theologians thus far because he openly admits that his own culture and experiences have profoundly shaped his knowledge of Christ and his theology, and he has recounted those experiences.

As an auxiliary soldier for the German air force in 1943, when Allied forces bombed his hometown of Hamburg in "Operation Gomorrah," he manned a battery with other troops. Amid the air raid, he watched his friend next to him be ripped apart by a bomb. Unscathed, Moltmann "got up and saw [his] friends and comrades all around [him] lying in shreds or dead." That night, out in the Black Forest, he surrendered to a British soldier. For the next three years he was a prisoner of war and perplexedly asked himself, "Why am I alive and not dead like the others?"

Witnessing war's brutality, he wondered, "Who is God?" As a prisoner in Scotland, he saw pictures of the Holocaust from Bergen-Belsen and Auschwitz for the first time. Afterward he wrote about himself and his fellow prisoners, "We saw ourselves mirrored in the eyes of the Nazi victims." Moltmann was horrified that he and his comrades had fought for such an insidious regime.[77]

Prison camp availed theological reflection for Moltmann. His disillusionment with war and life and the enduring shame and disgrace of German nationalism were met with God's own suffering, as Moltmann described it. He was not raised Christian, but in the Scottish prison an army chaplain gave the German soldiers copies of the Bible. The Psalms of lament and Jesus' own cry of abandonment, "My God, why have you forsaken me?" especially resonated in Moltmann's heart. Later, in 1947, he and other former prisoners of war were invited to a meeting where Dutch students told them of Christ's love. Jesus' own reconciliatory work was the healing bridge for the Germans and their former enemies. Accepting the gospel, Moltmann wrote, "For me that was an hour of liberation. I was able to breathe again, felt like a human being once more, and returned cheerfully to the camp behind the barbed wire."[78]

Following his wartime experiences, Moltmann studied theology in university. After his graduation he pastored a church for five years, but he spent the bulk of his career as a theology professor at the prestigious University of Tübingen. His own theology of hope, for which he is now famous, was inspired when he read the writings of the former Marxist philosopher Ernst Bloch (1885–1977).

Moltmann said that, even while from the Reformed tradition, all German theologians must come to terms with the theology of Martin Luther and his successor, Philipp Melanchthon (1497–1560), as well as the philosophy of Immanuel Kant (1724–1804) and Georg Wilhelm Friedrich Hegel (1770–1831). Moltmann's own academic development became important experiential grist for his theology, and through his education he embraced the history of the German intellectual tradition. To be Christ Jesus' disciples, Moltmann believes that we need to use both our hearts and our minds; and he celebrates the use of both. Today many call Moltmann the most important theologian of the twentieth century.

THE HOLY SPIRIT

Widely known as a theologian of hope, Moltmann believes together with Wolfhart Pannenberg that the End—God's future perfect reign—has broken into the present. Briefly, theologians capitalize *the End* to express that it is something *more*. It is more than life's cessation. It is certainly more than heaven. Even further, the End will be without end. The End is God's goal for creation's entirety: uninhibited justice, righteousness, and shalom—peace, every creature's flourishing, boundless joy, sinless beauty, untarnished relationship, and integrity. The End, Moltmann explains, was eminently manifested in Jesus' ministry and resurrection.

We can have hope because this ravaged world is not all there is. Not only does Moltmann believe that the End will be perfect and sublime (all Christians affirm that); he captures the human imagination by arguing that the End has invaded the present.

Jesus was who he was less for being a person with two natures, divinity and humanity, and more for his having brought the End with him. Indeed, Jesus' presence on earth initiated the dawn of the eschaton—sin's forgiveness, bodily wholeness, social dignity restored, and repaired relationship with God. Christians, then, are not merely waiting for the end of history, though they groan and yearn together in God's Spirit for that very thing, they also experience something of that now. When we experience the forgiveness of another person, that is a foretaste of the End. When we heal one another or laugh together, when we authentically treat people of different races or genders as equals, when we care for God's creation, and when we work to resolve suffering, we are participating in the character of the End.

In understanding Moltmann's work we might remind ourselves that much of Christian history, and more particularly Christian theology, has been characterized by Greek philosophy. The pre-Christian Greeks brilliantly conceptualized life as an interplay between, or an admixture of, spirit and matter. Some saw matter—physicality, form, and substance—as eternal. Others saw spirit—variously called mind, idea, or reason—as the only eternal element in the universe. Still others believed matter stemmed from and/or rudimentarily participated in the perfect realm of spirit; spirit gave rise to, or sustained, matter. The duality of spirit and matter was a worldview that helped the Greeks understand phenomena like human nature, beauty, altruism, and life's transcendent qualities—phenomena relegated to the spirit realm. It also helped ancient Greeks process other phenomena like harvest cycles, disease, destruction, and evil— phenomena relegated to the realm of matter.

Over the centuries this spirit-versus-matter duality was construed differently by various philosophers (post-Christian European Enlightenment philosophers were still playing with multiple variations on this theme), but that tandem was widely understood to precisely frame reality. When Christianity entered world history, the first Christian theologians, wanting to build bridges with people deeply interested in truth, contextualized the Christian message to fit this spirit-matter dualism. The issue for spirit-matter dualism was ontology, which comes from a Greek word connoting being and essence. If one asks what is the true nature of something, as theologians often do, one is asking a standard Greek ontological question.

For his part, Moltmann was one of several theologians who introduced a new and dynamic way of framing the Christian life.[79] Reality, at the foundational level, is not a matter-spirit duality but a matter of time and eternity. (With the Scripture's constant reference to God's own eternality, Jesus' and his apostles' teaching on eternal life, and the Bible's own prophetic visions of the End, we understand why many theologians are so excited about Moltmann's framework.) God, the timeless one, initiated reconciliation in and through Jesus Christ. Because he lives beyond time, God is free to bring the end of time with him into the present. In Jesus' earthly ministry the End manifested itself in things like physical healings, demon exorcisms, feeding the hungry, eating with social outcasts and the ritually unclean, and teaching women, and through those actions putting people in contact with God's Spirit.

We can have hope, Moltmann says, because God—in Jesus and his Spirit—has shown us his ultimate plans. God's plans are not to save merely our souls but our whole embodied selves. God is not looking to save us *from* the earth; he is looking to save us *with* the earth. In all of this, Moltmann's framework is this-life affirming. More specifically, he believes God loves each particular entity (human being, animal, plant). Poet Edna St. Vincent Millay (1892–1950) once wrote, "I love humanity but I hate people"; that is an abstraction of immense proportions. Moltmann does not want either love or life in the abstract. He argues repeatedly that God loves each particular creature and each particular creation in the universe. God's mission, and with it the mission of both Jesus and the Holy Spirit, is to bring life and affirm life to all. Life is not just what God *has* for either people or the earth. Life is who God *is*. Moltmann writes,

> The Gospel of John tells us quite simply what it is that is brought into the world from God through Christ: *life*. "I live, and you shall live also" (Jn. 14:19). For the Holy Spirit is "the source of life" and brings life into the world—whole life, full life, unhindered, indestructible, *everlasting* life. The creative and life-giving Spirit of God already brings this eternally living life here and now, before death, not just after death, because the Spirit brings Christ into this world and Christ is "the resurrection and the life" in person. . . . The sending of the Holy Spirit is the revelation of God's indestructible *affirmation* of life and his marvelous *joy* in life. Where Jesus is, there is life. . . . Where the Holy Spirit is present there is life.[80]

Like Karl Barth before him Moltmann affirms God's tri-une nature. In the Christian West, both Roman Catholic and Protestant, the Spirit has been construed as the love that flows between the Father and the Son. The Eastern Orthodox hold that the Son and the Spirit exist by virtue of their (eternal, not temporal) source, the Father. Both the East and the West assert that the three exist in relationship with one another, but the West has been criticized for its Trinitarian doctrine that tends to depersonalize the Spirit into the love shared by the Father and Son.

For his part Moltmann emphasizes a doctrine of the Trinity that is neither expressly Western nor Eastern, though his preference between those two falls with the latter. Moltmann embraces a position that is gaining more and more adherents worldwide: the three exist expressly in a relationship of *equality*. The Son is not subordinate to the Father, and the Spirit is not subordinate to the Son. Instead, and important for understanding some of his own novel positions, Moltmann asserts that *relationship is central* to God's own existence.[81]

God's own relationship was extended to creation and continues via the Holy Spirit's life-giving presence. Still, this is not pantheism—God is not the universe. Yet God is *in* the universe via his life-giving Spirit; this is called panentheism. Consequentially, for Moltmann God is an "open Trinity." Veli-Matti Kärkkäinen said of this model that in creation God "opens himself to the world and is also vulnerable to happenings in history."[82] God—open to and in relationship with the plurality that is himself—is also open to and in relationship with his creation. Moltmann's theology sees

God suffering due to the corrupted state of his creation. Repeatedly, Moltmann thus argues for both ecological stewardship and political liberation.

God, Moltmann reasons, is not some detached being who sits above his creation and watches it run its course, not at all perplexed whenever evil runs wild. To the contrary, God, in the biblical portrayal, loves his creation, intervenes in it and works diligently to preserve it. More central to Moltmann, God is love (1 Jn. 4:8). That he is so makes God vulnerable to that which he loves, precisely because love implies openness to the other.[83] Moltmann, in very daring language, says, "The suffering of a single innocent child is an irrefutable rebuttal of the notion of an almighty and kindly God in heaven. For a God who lets the innocent suffer and who permits senseless death is not worthy to be called God at all."[84] Elsewhere he states, "Creation's history of suffering is God's history of suffering too."[85] God suffers in every injustice, in every wound, and in every tragedy. And it is not just human suffering that grieves God, Moltmann also emphasizes the suffering of nature in his theology of the Holy Spirit.

On the one hand the Spirit's role, because he is the presence of God's life in creation, is to suffer with and alongside the hurting. "God is restless in his Spirit until he finds rest in us and in his world," Moltmann asserts.[86] The Spirit sighs, groans, and cries for final redemption (Rom. 8:26). Like a mother who gives birth to her children (and Moltmann is fond of calling the Spirit mother) the Spirit grieves in the midst of grief and cries in the midst of agony. The Spirit's role on the other hand is to continue to preserve and nourish life. Moroever, in the midst of evil and suffering the Spirit comes to bring us hope in Christ.

The Spirit is the well of life itself, the one who sustains the world, threatened as it is by nonbeing and annihilation.[87]

By freely choosing to create and remain in fellowship with his now fallen creation, God suffers. (This divine suffering is archetypal in Jesus' passion and crucifixion.) This view confirms Moltmann as a stalwart proponent of ecology. Life in developed countries—he does not put it succinctly, but Moltmann's regular criticisms of Western life, modernism, and the Charismatic movement make this evident—is destroying nature and exploiting the earth. Coincidingly, he notes that people are not just souls but bodies, and the pollution of the natural environment is bad for our bodies. Similar to nature religions that tenderly refer to the earth as "mother," people need to tenderly allow the earth its God-given Sabbath rest; the failure to stop this exploitation may mean the earth will "become desolate and void, and humanity will become extinct." God's Spirit gives us his energies and powers in order to contest life's violation. Anyone who is indifferent to the ecological system's destruction is an "ally of death."[88]

God's cosuffering, active through the Spirit's indwelling presence, also compassionately seeks to eradicate political and military destruction. Renowned for opposing nuclear proliferation and political domination of any kind, Moltmann widely advocates liberation theology: a perspective that seeks to bring justice to the oppressed. This proliferation emphasis makes Moltmann wary of all power, since in his thought power leads to abusiveness. Moltmann thus reasons that theologians should stop emphasizing Jesus' power as Lord and instead emphasize Jesus' love, freedom, and cosuffering as Lord. Through suffering, not violence, God is victorious over darkness and evil.[89]

The above concerns show that in his understanding of the Spirit Moltmann is a theologian who does not only live *in his head*. Frequently theologians construct beautiful and elaborate intellectual ideas that don't translate in ordinary life. Moltmann wants theology to matter in life as we live it, as we feel it in our hearts and bodies. To that end Moltmann values experience as a tremendous theological component. He openly admits that his wartime biography has shaped (we might say preshaped) the way he processes reality. Because experience is subjective, for many centuries theologians and philosophers were hesitant to include experience in their formulations, explanations, and worldviews. If self-knowledge is difficult to discover, how tentative should our statements about external reality be? Immanuel Kant especially emphasized the tentative nature of our knowing, and the era of modernism generally followed suit: objectivity—not subjectivity—is the goal in postulations about truth.

Representing a gigantic shift beyond modernism, Moltmann avers that, when people experience God's Spirit, circumstances and people change: "Human experience of God is the foundation of human theology." Experience for Moltmann is no longer something to apologize for, as the modernists did. *Experience is now a given*. Because the Spirit is the life-giver, because all life is rooted in God, all experience can be a vehicle for the Spirit.[90] The experience of God is not limited to Christian or churchly vehicles like the sacraments, the community of faith, or church rituals. Moltmann clarifies that the experience of God's Spirit is "an awareness of God in, with, and beneath the experience of life, which gives us an assurance of God's fellowship, friendship, and love."[91] A more holistic approach to life, Moltmann argues, includes our feelings and experiences. Further developing this idea, Moltmann explains that experiencing the Spirit is not only possible through charismatic gifts, although he believes they are legitimate. People should also look for the Spirit's presence in daily life and the physical creation.[92]

God's Spirit is at work in the Church but also in creation. When he describes the Spirit's work Moltmann uses words like *atmosphere, energy, energies, power,* and *force field.* For example, "In the Spirit God himself is present and surrounds us from every side. We live and breathe in God's atmosphere."[93] The Spirit makes us live *and* makes us feel more alive. Beautifully he wrote,

> When I love God I love the beauty of bodies, the rhythm of movements, the shining of eyes, the embraces, the feelings, the scents, the sounds of all this protean creation. When I love you my God, I want to embrace it all, for I love you with all my senses in the creations of your love. In all the things that encounter me, you are waiting for me. . . . The experience of God deepens the experiences of life. It does not reduce them. For it awakens the unconditional Yes to life. The more I love God, the more gladly I exist.[94]

ABIDING INFLUENCE

Moltmann's theology of the Holy Spirit is clearly shaped by his own experiences; again, he openly admits this. In fact, he explicitly states that we need to be aware of our experiential location as we do theology and follow Christ. Over the years this celebration of experience, this openness to God in life's different settings, has seen Moltmann involved in ecumenical (involving the whole Church, or for the sake of all Christians) conversations and endeavors around the world. He has shown himself willing to be open to the Holy Spirit in many, diverse places.

Moltmann is influential for reminding Christians we serve God in particular, historical times and specific geographic locations. Overwhelmed by the gravity of national or global problems, Christians forget that the Spirit yearns to live and work through us locally. Moltmann, with his Spirit-as-life-force emphasis, reminds us to be open to the presence of God's Spirit in the here and now. That kind of spatial and temporal location harkens to both Christ's incarnation and the Spirit's engifting actions. Jesus was not from everywhere or anywhere—he was from Nazareth; the particularity of Jesus speaks to God's love of each individual. The Holy Spirit gives different people different gifts for life and ministry; again, this is an affirmation of specificity and particularity. This *in-and-for-the-time-and-place* (technical theology calls this immanence; see Glossary) emphasis has theologians, pastors, and priests around the world reengaging their congregations and parishes with fresh energy and insight for the sake of relevancy. We cannot attribute theological relevancy solely to Moltmann, but he clearly represents a vanguard.

Particularly important for Moltmann, and this coincides with his emphasis on eschatology—the in-breaking of the future into the present—is his holistic approach to theology in general and his doctrine of God's Spirit in particular, which enable him to overcome the classical Greek dualism of spirit versus body. God is not merely trying to save our *souls*. He is at work to save the entirety of our beings. By interrupting the flow of history with the coming of Jesus and his Spirit, salvation has broken into the now in such a way that both the whole human person (body, soul, needs, relationships, hopes) and the whole creation have become the location for God's transforming actions. This places a new emphasis on physicality as a real site for encounter with God and can help Christians of all backgrounds seek to serve Christ for the sake of the here and now, and not just heaven or the afterlife. Again, this harkens to the incarnation itself: Jesus preached, ministered, healed, ate with, prophetically challenged, and comforted people in first-century Palestine. He was a specific man accomplishing God's specific purposes for and through him. God desires similarly for us.

Pastors and believers in underdeveloped countries particularly find Moltmann a robust dialogue partner. His emphasis on God's own suffering is strong medicine for those whose lives are characterized by severe poverty, neglect of diverse kinds, and political oppression. Especially before the collapse of the Soviet Union, Moltmann and other theologians who promoted theologies of hope caught the interest of other church leaders and scholars who were interested in freedom from political and economic oppression. This emphasis, especially in Latin America, gave rise to liberation theology. For his part Moltmann shared the concerns of liberation theologians even as he denied being one; other theologians view Moltmann as having a Neo-Marxist bent.[95] From the 1960s to the fall of Soviet Communism, liberation theology was a regular feature of magazine stories, academic seminars, and college courses. Closely aligned with political ideals that failed in society and economics, liberation theology has lost its former momentum.

Yet Moltmann will not be left behind so quickly! First, regarding our own study, his theology of the Spirit is indeed life affirming and nature affirming. With his aptitude for cosmic application, Moltmann's positions about God's Spirit provoke reflection and study by students and believers desiring to discern God's presence in daily life. Also important, and giving him an enduring voice, Moltmann writes with gripping verve and passion. He recognizes that theology speaks valuably to everyday life, thought, and values. Indeed, he attests that theology is exciting! Too often it's theologians who are boring. Because Moltmann incorporates a narrative and personal style of writing, and because he believes theology is ultimately about life itself, his influence will endure for generations.

The issue of style raises methodological questions. How is theology conducted? Among theologians, are there established rules or procedures? Scholars like Moltmann consider local and contextualized theologies and extrapolate their meanings for larger applications. There are others working diligently to construct and prescribe universal theories of reality, truth, and God and then overlay their meanings onto local contexts. Our next theologian, Wolfhart Pannenberg, a contemporary of Jürgen Moltmann's, represents this broader, and in some ways more traditional, trajectory.

9
Wolfhart Pannenberg
(1928–)

IS CHRISTIANITY merely a private affair between a
believer and God? Is religious faith something that is
true only for the members of a religion? Philosophers
of the Enlightenment—mid-seventeenth through
mid-nineteenth centuries—believed truth was true for
everyone; those philosophers assumed truth only needed
discovery and verification, and everyone everywhere naturally
would assent to its claims. Perspectives on truth shifted during
the modern philosophical era—late nineteenth through mid-
twentieth centuries. Modernism produced public tensions
between verifiable truth and private meaning. Verifiable truth,
the modernistic belief ran, is about factual evidence to which
everyone assents: the law of gravity is true for people in both
Ukraine and Uganda. Religion, modernistic thinking asserted,
is about private values isolated to personal meaning: Jesus might
be Lord and true for a Texas rancher, but not for a Yemeni
carpet salesman. (That *all* facts are interpreted, constructed,
and maintained by large plausibility structures—alternatively

called metanarratives: cultures, beliefs, philosophies, and religions—is openly recognized by our current postmodern philosophical era. Facts and values are not so distinct as modernists held.)

Generally, Christians went along with modernism's fact-value dichotomy. Christians often labeled as conservatives made Christianity a private affair because they lived more cloistered lives, lives that precluded dialogue with modern philosophies; these Christians did not intentionally interface with society, so their version of Christianity was secluded from larger truth considerations. For their part, Christians often labeled as liberal made Christianity a private affair for philosophical reasons we saw in Friedrich Schleiermacher: persons can subjectively experience God, Christianity heightens God-consciousness, and we can internally know God. This subjective tendency, embraced by these Christians, assisted modernism's fact-value dichotomy: religion was about personal values, values dissected from larger truth questions.

Despite the influence of modernism's fact-value dichotomy, today there remain Christians who still assert that all truth is God's truth: truth is true for everyone, or else it isn't true at all. Religious truth for these Christians does not operate with a different set of rules than scientific truth. If religion is true it will be verifiable and public, not secluded in personalized categories. This perspective, the classical approach, is more encompassing of life, science, and reality than the modernistic view. One theologian who believes theology must facilitate a comprehensive and public view of Christian truth is Wolfhart Pannenberg.

Born in Poland, Pannenberg was baptized a Lutheran as a
baby. Despite that event, he rarely attended church during his
childhood in Germany. He had an intense religious experience
as a boy, but Pannenberg's proclivities were more philosophical
than experiential: while only an adolescent he studied great
philosophers and religious thinkers. Remarkably, as a high school
student, Pannenberg decided that Christianity was the most
philosophically sound religion.[96] His hunger to learn naturally led
to a university education. While at university in Basel, Pannenberg
studied under Karl Barth; important for our study, he disagreed
with Barth that God's revelation cannot be found in the world
of nature. Later, Pannenberg earned a PhD in theology at the
University of Heidelberg. He is today a theological giant. Lutheran
in background (and thus committed to Lutheran categories
of God's revelation) but conversant with a sweeping range of
ideas, Pannenberg's insistence that theological truth needs to be
integrated with disciplines outside religious categories, such as
philosophy, history, and the sciences, is discussed, if not wrestled
with, by theologians around the world. Though today retired,
Pannenberg's authoritative positions on particular issues such
as Christology and revelation are studied by theologians across
various traditions. To better understand the nuance of his doctrine
of the Holy Spirit, we must first turn to some of Pannenberg's
fundamental commitments.

THE HOLY SPIRIT

Everything that has existence does so in and because of God's
Spirit, according to Pannenberg, who believes God is the

"power that determines everything." Since God gives existence to everything, theology should *be* about everything. While it is true that we cannot know anything perfectly or exhaustively, even with the help of the sciences, we must, however, use all the "energies and faculties we have to state what we can state in our time."[97] Characterized as we are by our location in time and space, our truth assertions will be imperfect and tentative. Nevertheless, we must still seek to be faithful to the idea of objective truth.

Pannenberg also believes that human beings are naturally religious: it is reasonable, Pannenberg claims, that the creator would have left his mark on the creation. Yet for Pannenberg this does not prove God's existence. Other world religions represent how differing peoples process their awareness of the infinite in life, while this intuitive awareness does not itself constitute knowledge of God. Nevertheless, it may be that God's Spirit is at work in saving ways in other religions. (Despite his generosity toward other religions Pannenberg refutes universalism.[98]) Still, he affirms that Jesus Christ alone is God's saving revelation.

Foundational to his theology is Pannenberg's belief that revelation is something God alone does and gives. (Here he follows Karl Barth.) We cannot establish a relationship with God on our own. The world religions are all locked in a struggle for supremacy, and the one that best accounts for and illumines all reality eventually will win out. Pannenberg believes the revelation of Jesus Christ is that superior religion.

Together with his former teaching colleague Jürgen Moltmann, Pannenberg maintains that the End—God's future perfect reign—has broken into the present with the coming of

Jesus and the Spirit. We are not simply waiting for the End. We can have hope in the present because we know there is more. Because Jesus initiated the entrance of God's kingdom in history, we know God has something more—now—for his creation and us: the presence of the End.

History is important to Pannenberg for many reasons:

- It is the realm for God's revelation; God reveals himself through actions and words.
- It is the realm where the adherents of various religions experience God, interpret those experiences, and subsequently contend about truth claims.
- It is critical to theological formulation; history's observable quality makes truth claims public and open to scrutiny—this public and verifiable nature of history is foundational both for theological formulation and all truth claims.

Methodologically, Pannenberg holds that amid the human quest for truth reason is paramount. Truth cannot simply be established through authority; just because someone with pedigree asserts something does not make it true. Similarly, truth cannot simply be established through a vote; on particular matters, the majority can be wrong. Reason, a tool available to all, enables scrutiny and public verification. Pannenberg's emphasis on reason leads him to argue that theology, like all approaches to truth, needs to cohere with all other means of human knowing. Reason enables consensus-building concerning universal truth.[99] Having established some of Pannenberg's fundamental commitments will bring clarity to his teaching on the Holy Spirit.

For centuries Christian theology has held to a doctrine of immanence—that God is in and through his creation—using Christology, the study of Jesus Christ's person and work. Scriptures like John 1:3, "All things came into being through Him, and apart from Him nothing came into being that has come into being," and Colossians 1:17, "He is before all things, and in Him all things hold together," are foundational to this approach. Jesus is the Logos (cf., John's Gospel and 1 John)— the reason, order, information, and life—that permeates the universe. God abides in and through life, Christian theology has traditionally asserted, through Christ's cosmic presence.

By way of contrast Pannenberg prefers to speak of God's Spirit as the means of immanence. (For further nuance, see Glossary.) Bible passages sustaining this perspective include Genesis 2:7, "Then the LORD God formed man of dust from the ground, and breathed into his nostrils the breath of life; and man became a living being," and Psalm 104:29–30, "You take away their spirit, they expire, / and return to their dust. / You send forth Your Spirit, they are created; / And You renew the face of the ground" (cf. Job 12:10; 34:13–15). Keeping fidelity to the Bible, Pannenberg does not simply cite Scripture verses to state his positions. He works with a fully developed theological system, not least of which is his understanding of the Trinity.

In biblical terms, the Spirit is the breath of God. The notion of an all-pervasive breath that animates life makes great sense to Pannenberg. The Spirit as breath nicely accords with the development of field theory in natural science, and as we noted above, Pannenberg cares that theology illumine all reality and knowledge. Field theory holds that all things exist in a space-time-material-energy field. Briefly put, Pannenberg holds that this energy field is in reality God's Spirit. All creatures, even all nonsentient life-forms (e.g., plants, bacteria, viruses), participate in the environment that is God's Spirit. All creatures participate in and are dependent on God's life-giving Spirit without themselves therefore becoming God; God's creations have a level of independence.[100]

Field theory is an enormous shift from Newtonian mechanics. In Newton's model, every entity—creature, thing, outcome—has a cause; for example, children are caused by parents, who had parents, and so on. In Newton's model God was relegated to a kind of *watchmaker* role: he put the universe together, wound its springs (i.e., gave it natural laws), and allows it to run its course without his further involvement.

Field theory, however, views life more in terms of mutual interconnectivity, and Pannenberg's doctrine of the Spirit, using the relational elements of existence, sees the Holy Spirit as the "power that determines everything."[101] God doesn't just create things and then leave them alone. God is present in and through everything, constantly causing them to be. If they are alive, they are only so through the Spirit. Still more, the Spirit of God, as the energy field in which everything exists, is also the power of God that orients creatures toward the End. We see signposts of this, Pannenberg says, in creatures' ability to transcend themselves and move beyond their own immediate environments. All things are moving, by the Spirit's power, toward the final God-appointed End, the perfect future where God will be "all in all" (1 Cor. 15:28). Or, to see Pannenberg's position from another perspective, the Spirit is not just the present-time life giver. The Spirit not only sustains life now; he is also the one pulling all beings toward the perfect completion of time and being: the End.[102] God's Spirit thus has an eschatological role: he constantly draws this broken and perverted world toward the future, toward the God-ordained perfection of the new heavens and the new earth.

Our study has revealed a constant Protestant emphasis on the Holy Spirit's subjective or existential work. Wesley, Schleiermacher, Kuyper, Barth, and Williams each emphasized the subjective work the Spirit accomplishes in believers. Whether it be drawing sinners to Christ, illuminating the biblical text, enabling faith, or empowering for mission, the Spirit is critical to God's purposes. Particularly concerning people's appropriation of God's truth, Pannenberg represents a significant departure from established Protestant theology.

As noted before, Pannenberg believes truth is true for everyone, everywhere. Committed to that classical, premodern, notion of truth, Pannenberg maintains an untraditional theory of the Spirit's work in our knowing God's truth: we do *not* need the Spirit to understand the truth of the gospel. Reason is enough; we don't need the Spirit to assist our minds or illumine God's truth. Stanley Grenz, Pannenberg's student in Munich, summarizes his mentor, "He tolerates no suggestion that some additional inspired word or some supernatural working of the Spirit must be added to events. Meaning arises out of the events themselves." For Pannenberg, truth is true for all people, and history is accessible for all people. (This also means Pannenberg does *not* maintain the classical distinctions between general and special revelation;[103] people can ascertain truth about God in a multitude of ways.) Why someone does not or does come to faith is *not* the result of the Spirit's working. Pannenberg holds that the reason some come to faith and some do not is a mystery owing to human personhood.[104]

This does not mean that Pannenberg entirely excludes the Spirit's role in salvation. He avers that God's Spirit sweeps aside prejudgments that prevent a person from *rationally engaging* in the historical event. But the Spirit does this, Pannenberg asserts, *from within* the event, not from the outside as an external force or special illumination. In this way Pannenberg maintains both his doctrine of the Spirit of God's indwelling of all things— the Spirit works inside the event, not as an external force or dynamic—and his belief that all truth is rationally discernible by everyone.

Despite Pannenberg's using the scientific concept of field theory to explain God's Spirit, he does believe the Spirit is a person, not an impersonal force. The Father, Son, and Spirit are persons in God and are persons who are God. Pannenberg therefore follows classic Christian doctrine in considering God a triune being. His nuanced position, however, is that there is no subordination in the Trinity. Neither the Son nor the Spirit are inferior to the Father. Indeed, the Father's kingdom is only realized through the persons of the Spirit and the Son. In Jesus' conception, baptism, and resurrection, he received the Spirit, and when Jesus ascended to heaven he sent the Spirit; all of this implies mutuality and relationship. The unity of God is not derived from the Father, as Eastern Orthodoxy asserts, but through the three persons' mutual relatedness.

Another of Pannenberg's nuanced positions is that the Church is the creation of both Christ Jesus and the Spirit. Clearly challenging our Western contemporary era's hyper-individualism, Pannenberg teaches that the Spirit comes not only for individual believers' sake but also for the Church's sake. Luke shows this in Acts 2:1–11, where the Spirit rested on each believer yet did so for the edification of everyone present. So, Pannenberg argues, the Spirit works in and through the Church as one body, not just individual believers.

The Church needs characterization by both Jesus and the Spirit, Pannenberg maintains, but over the centuries it has preferred Jesus. That Jesus-centered model has seen churches and institutions place too much emphasis on hierarchy and organizational structure (i.e., men alone serving in Jesus' place, establishing channels of authority). More recently, Pannenberg notes, those churches that emphasize the Holy Spirit as their exclusive source tend toward harmful overexuberance. The Church needs both Jesus and the Spirit as its foundation. This Jesus-and-Spirit emphasis mirrors Pannenberg's commitments to the mutual relations of the Trinity and his belief that all truth is interrelated.

ABIDING INFLUENCE

As with the other twentieth-century theologians this book surveys, it is difficult to precisely assess Pannenberg's immediate influence. Still, Panneberg is representative of important shifts.

The Spirit as the divine force field that determines everything is a fascinating way of constructing the issue. This view affirms the classical Christian commitment to the Spirit's life-giving nature, and does so in a relevant way. Theology that builds bridges to and engages the regnant worldview makes penetration and transformation of that worldview possible. But it remains to be seen whether global Christians will be drawn to a notion of the Spirit as life-giver who moves us toward *future* perfection. Christendom's overwhelming majority (Roman Catholics, Eastern Orthodox, and Protestants of most stripes) sees the Spirit as more active in the believer's life *now* concerning the renewal of hearts and minds, together with processes like illumination, guidance, and instilling godly values.

Because of his emphasis on the in-breaking of God's kingdom within the plane of history, and because of Pannenberg's emphasis on the importance of history in general, our present lives are open to the possibility of God's transformation. We need not only hope for what will happen in the afterlife, or the end of history, because God seeks to bring change now. Currently there are cynics who believe that history is merely a matter of the accounts that are—as is so commonly said in university classes—"written by the winners." Such cynics aver there is no history that is universally true for everyone; there are, it follows, only histories: localized stories relevant only to particular people. Against such cynicism Pannenberg offers a hopeful perspective: God really does act and reveal himself in history. Indeed, God has changed history's trajectory via Jesus' life, ministry, death, and resurrection. God's work in history is true for everyone and applies to everyone; the human history is thus interwoven with God himself.

Among contemporary European theologians Pannenberg is a rationalist. Some theologians, in fact, have accused him of being a hyper-rationalist. His understanding of Christian truth as being accessible to people apart from the Spirit's illumination, his belief that all truth is accessible through reason, and his belief that history itself is the medium of God's presence and revelation in history all bear out his rationalist bent. Theoretically, Pannenberg's framing of theology as one of the many ways to access truth allows theology to be respected by academics and intellectuals. Moreover, this emphasis on the universality of reason allows for the possibility of Christian dialogue among the many academic disciplines and also makes room for interface with the adherents of other religions. Theologians have long been interested in science, but they have not always been ready to engage the intuitions and discoveries of science. Pannenberg represents a theology invigorated by new discussions with these other disciplines. (Whether the other disciplines themselves are interested or eager for dialogue with theology is another matter!)

Many Christians would share Pannenberg's emphases on maintaining fidelity to the major biblical themes and on reason, even though those Christians might be alarmed by his criticisms of classical Christianity and traditional piety and by his belief that God may be working in other religions. Like Pannenberg, many also hold that theology needs an apologetic (reasoned defense of the faith) quality; we are free to persuade people for the sake of the gospel. After all, the apostle Paul persuaded people for the sake of Christ and his gospel (Acts 18:4, 13; 2 Cor. 5:11). And God's revelation, we are told in the Bible, pierces the human heart and places claims on people (Heb. 4:12); the Bible doesn't apologize for its own persuasive tack. So this willingness to engage the world and all the means of knowledge—including rationalism—with Christian faith commitments appeals to many. Other theologians, though, wonder if Pannenberg's method is overcommitted to both reason and history. Whether his positions can endure in a world that increasingly embraces nonrational means of being and knowing, and whether his quest for objective and universal truth can abide this historic shift, remain to be seen.

Less rationalistic and less apologetic (less committed to universal reason) is our next theologian, Clark Pinnock. Profoundly influenced by both Jürgen Moltmann and Wolfhart Pannenberg, Pinnock fascinatingly represents how quickly these enormous shifts are occurring within theology, not least of which concerning God's Spirit.

10
Clark Pinnock
(1937–2010)

*T*HE TWENTIETH CENTURY saw more cross-fertilization within Christendom than any previous century; and much of that change was rooted in and around the Holy Spirit. Pentecostalism and the Charismatic renewal, two movements driven by a focus on the Spirit, profoundly enhanced this cross-fertilization, as great traditions like Roman Catholicism and Anglicanism and mainline Protestant denominations—such as Methodists, Presbyterians, and Lutherans—were conditioned by dynamic spiritual experiences. This cross-fertilization was also certainly facilitated by virtue of the electronic media; interested leaders could almost immediately learn about new churchly developments outside their own domain.

Another twentieth-century development, the ecumenical movement, also caused cross-fertilization. Many church leaders believe the Holy Spirit is God's motivating force helping different tributaries of Christendom to learn about one another, treat one another respectfully, and even work together at

missional or societal levels.[105] Jesus himself had prayed to his
Father, "that they may be one even as We are" (Jn. 17:11, 21,
22). Ecumenism (stemming from the Greek word meaning, "for
the whole house") is an impulse to help the whole Church—
Roman Catholics, Eastern Orthodox, and Protestants—come
together. First started in 1910, the ecumenical movement had
high hopes of visible unity: all Christians would come together
in and as one body. Regarding visible unity, those hopes have
been dashed, but churches are indeed still learning kindness and
patience with the *other*.[106]

Despite what some church leaders prefer, the cross-fertilization
continues. One may attend a Roman Catholic Mass and find the
congregation singing charismatic Vineyard worship songs. One
may attend an emergent church[107] and participate in a very liturgical ceremony accompanied by incense. Protestant churches are
beginning to house Eastern Orthodox icons, and Anglicans hold
their own charismatic church services. The different spirituali-
ties and cultures of Christendom are mixing, reinvigorating one
another, and producing new flavors in new contexts. The same
reinvigoration is occurring at theological levels.

Pentecostals are exploring patristic theology.[108] Roman
Catholics, touched by their interface with Pentecostals, are
reexploring the Holy Spirit–driven spirituality of the ancient
church.[109] Protestants are moving past the polemic of the sixteenth-century Reformation and beginning to learn what they
hold in common theologically with both the ancient church and
contemporary Roman Catholics.[110] A theologian who exemplified this cross-fertilization was Clark Pinnock. Born and raised
in the Baptist tradition in Canada, Pinnock went on to embrace

and then teach Evangelical doctrine and theology. Initially he wrote books on biblical authority and apologetics.[111] Over time, however, his interests broadened, and he explored new avenues of theology, writing books on the openness of God,[112] annihilationism,[113] and salvation.[114] These books caused him to come under suspicion by more ardent Calvinists committed to God's absolute sovereignty and the doctrine of biblical inerrancy (i.e., that the Bible contains no errors of any kind; even when it speaks to issues of science it is 100 percent accurate). Even as a committed Calvinist Evangelical (see Glossary), Pinnock represented the cross-fertilization by moving to embrace positions held by Arminian Protestants, Eastern Orthodox, and even Roman Catholics.

As his ecumenical work continued, he broke ranks with Calvinist Evangelicals on the work of the Holy Spirit. Many Calvinists believe that the Holy Spirit's miraculous activities flourished during the time of the apostles but that those signs and wonders ceased after the apostolic era; those who hold this position are called cessationists. Attending the Toronto Airport Vineyard as a careful observer of the movement of the Holy Spirit, Pinnock experienced the Holy Spirit and felt constrained to reconsider his theology in light of it. Healed of an eye affliction, he said, "I know from personal experience that one such incident can be worth a bookshelf of academic apologetics for Christianity (including my own books)." Experiences of God can reorient entire worldviews. Upon seeing a vision of God near death, the medieval theologian Thomas Aquinas (AD 1224–74) similarly said that he could write no more, "All that I have written now seems like straw."

THE HOLY SPIRIT

In his book *Flame of Love* Pinnock examined theology from the vantage point of the Spirit.[115] Traditional systematic theologies first categorize and then explore different topics. Often a given theology moves sequentially through the Bible's own revelation: God, creation, human nature, the fall and sin, Jesus Christ, salvation, and the afterlife. Traditionally, chapters about the Spirit are distinct, and theological categories are rarely interwoven. (The more integrated a theology, the more other scholars view it as systematic.) For instance, many Protestant theologies will take salvation as an all-encompassing rubric and then strain other topics through that interpretive sieve. In a unique move, Pinnock took the Holy Spirit as the commitment informing all his topics under study: Trinity, creation, Christology, church, union with God, universality, and truth. Rather than a solely rational approach to God's Spirit, Pinnock maintained that understanding also calls for contemplative openness. Pinnock said in *Flame of Love* that he was intentionally being creative, innovative, and exploratory, writing, "The Spirit makes us open to new horizons and new possibilities. We are empowered with hope to transcend situations and limitations. Therefore it is important to experience the Spirit and reflect on our experience." In fascinating ways Pinnock's own theological approach coincided with his understanding of the Spirit as creative, innovative, and playful.

Like Moltmann and Pannenberg before him, Pinnock affirmed the Trinity as the essential commitment of Christian life and then proceeded from that doctrine. His model of

the Trinity was a social one: the three persons are equal.
Particularly, he followed Irenaeus, a second-century theologian
who proposed that the Son and the Spirit are the two hands of
God the Father working in creation and salvation. The Son is
not subordinate to the Spirit, and the Spirit is not subordinate
to the Son; Pinnock believed too many historic theologians
had embraced Trinitarian models purporting subordination.
Instead, the Son and Spirit complement one another and work
together. Agreeing with one classical Trinitarian position,
Pinnock concurred with Augustine: the Spirit is the bond of
love between the Father and the Son. The same bond of love
uniting the Son and Father comes to human persons and draws
them into Trinitarian love.[116] In Pinnock's thinking, creation
and salvation are elements of the same dynamic: the love of
God moving out to creation. Pinnock said, "Almost everything
else I will have occasion to say [in this book] will spring from
this ontology. Spirit is essentially the serendipitous power of
creativity, which flings out a world in ecstasy and simulates
within it an echo of the inner divine relationships, *ever seeking
to move God's plans forward*."[117] This forward-propelling quality of
the Spirit harkens to something theologians call teleology: the
God-given goal or end of things. It is particularly the Spirit
who moves creatures toward their goal. And the goal always
concerns union with God.

In Pinnock's Trinitarian model the Spirit is both what God
has and *is*. The Father and Son *have*, that is share, the Holy
Spirit. Yet, God *is* Spirit. Jesus said, "God is Spirit" (Jn. 4:24).
Following Pannenberg, Pinnock believed the Spirit is a field of
deity. Indeed, all three persons are Spirit, all three share in the

Godhead. This is because God is a being in relationship. He enjoys union among himself (awkward though that may sound to our ears) as Father, Son, and Spirit. God's goal is to extend that shared union to others beyond himself. Christ's redemption accomplishes that union, Pinnock averred, but so did creation. Redemption heals sin's rupture between God and humanity, and by creating, God began to share life with formerly nonexistent beings. Love itself/himself, God shares with others and invites them into his union.

Like Barth and other theologians in this survey, Pinnock believed we cannot limit Spirit—regularly Pinnock simply used Spirit, not "Holy" or "the"; apparently he believed this would help us imagine the Spirit as both a person and a force—as "an ornament of piety." God's Spirit is not an added extra for Christian piety—by that criticism, Pinnock apparently targeted Charismatics for limiting the Spirit's role to personal piety. Rather, the Bible reveals Spirit as the giver of life. Spirit was there in the beginning, brooding "over the primeval waters" and "turning chaos into cosmos."[118] Truly, Spirit approaches Christians for more than piety. The Spirit is God himself, the fountain of life.

Too much Christian theology and piety is characterized by a secular-sacred split, according to Pinnock. (On this he agreed with the long-standing liturgical perspective of sacramental traditions.) The secular-sacred split viewpoint holds that some things believers do cooperate with God's sacred purposes for life, while other, rather mundane and secular, things believers do are inconsequential to God's purposes. Prayer, church attendance, Bible reading, and receiving the sacraments are categorized as sacred practices for most Christians. Conversely, dish washing, driving to work, eating meals, and paying bills are categorized as secular. Instead, Pinnock argued that *all* of it matters to God, *all* of it is sacred, because Spirit is present in and through all of life. Life's entirety, not just the supposedly sacred things we do, is a meaningful gift from God.

More alarmingly, Pinnock said, a secular-sacred split characterizes the way we think about ourselves as human beings: we see our souls as important and eternal and our bodies as necessary but fleeting and less significant. If we see Spirit as giving and sustaining all life, including our physical bodies, we will be less likely to devalue physicality or time on this side of eternity. Pinnock held that temporal physicality is the realm in and through which God has revealed himself. Jesus' birth and ministry occurred in and through a human body, in time. Spirit raised Jesus' body. Spirit calls believers together as Christ's body. All of this temporal-physicality is possible because Spirit—life's very source—enables it to live and move.

Pinnock built on the concept of temporal-physicality: the new creation that is Christ's redemption (i.e., salvation, resurrection, glorification) always presupposes the original creation (human nature and human bodies). So too the human spirit's life and existence presupposes the Holy Spirit's life and existence. Spirit takes the temporal-physical creature and enhances it. Alternately stated, redemption is not about leaving this world behind but is about renewing this world and raising it to a new and more beautiful level.

Pressed on the point about Spirit's presence, Pinnock said, "Theology would not think of denying the omnipresence of God but may overlook the omnipresence of the Spirit." Christians may discuss together God's omnipresence, but they rarely consider that it is Spirit who is omnipresent. God is present everywhere as the Spirit of the Trinity. Wherever there is life there is Spirit. Wherever there is life, the same Spirit who is united to Father and Christ is present. Consequently Pinnock asserted, "The power of love is at work everywhere in the world, not just in churches. The redeeming God is the Creator God. There is a unity to God's work in nature and history, not a dualism."[119] Churches do not own or possess God's Spirit; rather, they are owned and possessed by him.

Because of Spirit's presence, creation itself is a kind of sacrament: God's relational love, existing before creation's beginning, is present in and through temporal-physicality. All of life stems *from* God. But life—physical, temporal, common, everyday life— also *conveys* God. God, relational and playful, made room for others (the universe, beings, people, animals, etc.) to exist. Not for the sake of his own fulfillment did God make room for others. God does not need or yearn to be glorified. Instead—as an expression of the love that eternally belongs to him as Father, Son, and Spirit—God gave life when he created, and God sustains life today.

Pinnock more strenuously emphasized Spirit as life-giver: not only is Spirit present as life-giver, he is involved in the details of creation. It follows that he is active in life's natural processes, a dynamic that speaks to the dialogue between theology and science precisely because they are interested in the same subject matter, even if they each study it from different vantage points. Theology explains the beauty and the progression of life via

God's Spirit, and Pinnock averred that science explains beauty and the progression of life via evolution. Pinnock desired to ease the purported tension between science and Christianity, and like Pannenberg he viewed discussions of God's Spirit as a relief from this tension. As theology needs science, science needs theology. Here Pinnock quoted Albert Einstein, "Religion without science is blind—science without religion is lame."[120]

The Spirit in Pinnock's theology is not singularly about life processes. Spirit is also critical for Christology.[121] (In the late twentieth century, scholars labeled this emphasis Spirit-Christology.) Pinnock astutely reminded us that Jesus himself was the God-ordained Messiah because of the Spirit. The biblical Greek word *christos* means "anointed one," anointed of the Spirit. Jesus was eternally God, but it was Spirit that made him Christ: the one who accomplishes God's mission. The Spirit overshadowed Jesus' birth, but the Gospels clarify that Spirit also empowered Jesus for ministry, enabling him to perform signs and wonders. Indeed, so central was Spirit to his ministry that blaspheming the Spirit, Jesus said, was a sin leading to damnation (Matt. 12:32). Spirit enabled Jesus to conquer darkness. Spirit raised Christ from the dead. Clearly, the Spirit and Jesus are the two hands of God not only in creation and the work of salvation (i.e., atonement) but in Jesus' very self and identity. Pinnock said, "The point to stress here is that the Spirit is more central to the story of Jesus than theology has usually acknowledged."[122] Even in Jesus' earthly life, the Spirit was key in the work of God. This emphasis, while biblical, differs from most Protestant theology.

One of Spirit-Christology's strengths regards application for individual Christians: it's a powerful story. God wants to accomplish in us and through us what he accomplished in and through Jesus of Nazareth. Spirit empowered Jesus and Spirit yearns to empower us. Spirit heightened Jesus' awareness of and dependence on God his Father, and he desires to similarly attune us. Spirit worked redemptively in and through Jesus, and he similarly wants us to become redemptive coworkers. Salvation is a Spirit event for Pinnock, not just a Christ event. Tethered to the biblical witness, Spirit-Christology motivates Christians for service and mission.

The doctrine of the Church, too, garnered a Spirit-permeation in Pinnock, and here we see his ecumenical character radiating. Over the centuries, Catholics especially have reasoned that the Church universal is the continuation of Christ's incarnation. Pinnock argued it is more accurate to say the Church is the continuation of Jesus' anointing, not his incarnation. The incarnation pertains to Christ's nature: he was both human and divine. Anointing pertains to the Spirit's presence and power in and through Jesus; believers' participation in a similar dynamic is possible.

Consistent with his belief that God's Spirit, as life-giver, works sacramentally within all of life, Pinnock believed that the local church itself can be a sacrament and convey grace. (Overwhelmingly, most Protestants are not sacramental, and those who are limit sacramentality to the Lord's Supper and water baptism.) Pinnock built on his doctrine of the Holy Spirit and expanded his notions of sacramentality with God's triune life. The relational, triune God extends his own union to the Church, Christ's body. Christians experience God's sacramental presence when two or three are gathered together in his name

(Matt. 18:20); so the gathering itself is a means of grace. Yet Pinnock prodded further. In God's presence, many liturgical elements serve Spirit's grace-giving purposes: dance, the use of various colors, banners, dramas, festivals, processions, incense, together with the charismatic gifts (e.g., prophecy, speaking in tongues, healings). Pinnock's ecumenical impulses shined in his doctrine of the Church.

That Christians gather together to worship and celebrate Christ as the Church matters in Pinnock's Spirit-doctrine, but so does the mission of the Church. The Spirit impels the Church to gather followers and transform them into disciples; provoked by the Spirit, disciples subsequently will transform society and culture. In his ministry, Jesus established the Church's missional agenda. Jesus' mission was not implementing a slick, gimmicky program; it was following the Spirit's guidance and obeying the Father. For Pinnock, these truths meant the Church doesn't determine her mission, God does.

As earlier intimated, with Pinnock's belief that the Spirit works sacramentally throughout life, God is neither bound to Christianity nor the institution of the Church. Pinnock insisted that the ever-present God wants to save everyone (Zech. 14:9; 1 Tim. 2:4), so God "always reach[es] out to sinners." How does Spirit do this? Through general revelation. General revelation is knowledge about God gained through studying his creation: history, human conscience, beauty, order, design, and morality. Pinnock maintained that God's Spirit works redemptively—not just in life-giving or life-sustaining ways—but through general revelation "God is always reaching out to sinners by the Spirit. There is no general revelation or natural knowledge of God that is not at the same time gracious revelation and a *potentially saving knowledge*. All revealing and reaching out are rooted in God's grace and are aimed at bringing sinners home." Moreover, Pinnock believed that for too long traditional theology has driven a wedge between creation and redemption. "Access to grace," he said, is "less of a problem for theology when we consider it from the standpoint of Spirit, because whereas Jesus bespeaks particularity, Spirit bespeaks universality. The incarnation occurred in a thin slice of land in Palestine, but its implications touch the farthest star."[123] Particularity does not make Christ irrelevant; Jesus was God's gift to the whole human race. Contemporary relevance resided in Pinnock's theology of the Spirit; God's ability to reach out and draw people into union with himself is unlimited. While he may have not known *how* Spirit is at work in other religions, Pinnock trusted that God truly works inside them.

ABIDING INFLUENCE

As we saw with Moltmann and Pannenberg, assessing recent theologians' influence is a knotty task. It is far easier to suggest where they participate in the larger surrounding forces. Viewing them as templates, as suggestive prototypes, helps us better discern what is occurring within Christendom.

Among Western Christian scholars, and expanding the net to include many Roman Catholics, a growing theological migration sees Christianity moving beyond mere forgiveness of sins. Reinvigorated studies of ancient (patristic) Christianity often share this concern; the patristic fathers (e.g., Irenaeus, Origen, Clement of Alexandria, Athanasius) said genuine life in Christ involves creation's grandest elements together with the mundane dimensions of human life. Those ancients called the doctrine *theosis*: the complete transformation of personal identity and being through sharing in God's identity and being. Studies of historic Christian mystics and the Eastern Orthodox church similarly manifest this impulse to surpass salvation as the singular Christian concept. By emphasizing union with God, Pinnock shared this larger theological readjustment.

Blurring the categories of creation and redemption, something Pinnock ardently supported, also occurs among other recent theologians and helps believers move beyond the oft-assumed secular-sacred split. Indeed, the Holy Spirit is God's means of omnipresence. The value in joining creation and redemption allows us to be more respectful of and sensitive to all manner of life, not least of which includes the globe's poor and disaffected. Pinnock's shift also aids in seeing as valuable life's common, ordinary, and even boring elements.

Nevertheless when the Spirit as life-giver is expanded to broadly imply that God works redemptively apart from the preaching of the gospel, the presence of Christ in churches (i.e., witness, service, sacraments), and/or the particularity of Jesus Christ, we have moved beyond the apostolic witness about the Spirit; so argue other theologians. Few theologians would argue against the notion that Jesus died and rose again for everyone. Yet some theologians see Pinnock's proposal that atonement occurs through some ambiguous presence of the Spirit as passing beyond the biblical teaching.

The ecumenical cross-fertilization of Pinnock's thought is part of a substantial theological movement. Increasingly, believers enjoy learning about Christian traditions different from their own. Globalization places different people together and sees them doing business together in novel ways. Christian ecumenism fosters its own novel version of mutuality: believers seek and celebrate commonalities before they begin to focus on one another's distinctions. Reaching out to different Christian theological traditions, Pinnock exemplified a more inclusive attitude.

Pinnock's theology of God's Spirit is also noteworthy, if only for his method: putting the Spirit at the front of, or in the center of, the theological enterprise. Many new approaches to theology are budding around the world. Increasingly, theologians are producing integrative theorizing with the help of newer philosophies, rhetorical studies, sociological tools of analysis, and participatory observation. Our next chapter's theologian, Michael Welker, is fascinating not just because he sees the biblical witness as both a guiding standard and an accepted source for theological investigation but because he sees so much that is new within long-studied Christian documents.

11
Michael Welker
(1947–)

*I*S THERE SUCH A THING as absolute truth? Does changeless truth exist for everyone in every place and time? During the seventeenth through twentieth centuries, philosophers in particular and Western society in general believed the answer to those questions was yes. The broad assumption was that capital–*T* truth existed, we just need to determine how to locate, access, and define it. And so philosophy during those three hundred years was on a quest to locate and anchor human knowing in absolute truth. (Fascinatingly, conservative Protestants similarly grasped for certitude by arguing that the Bible was completely without error precisely when conservative Roman Catholics were asserting the pope can never err on matters of faith and doctrine—both groups responding to the larger philosophical pressure about certainty of human knowing.)

Exercising apparent irony, René Descartes (1596–1650) attempted to anchor knowledge's certainty in doubt. We don't know everything perfectly, reasoned Descartes, but it is impossible to doubt that we doubt; he represented an intellectual approach to truth labeled rationalism. John Locke (1632–1704) took another approach, believing experience is the foundation of truth. We are able to note, measure, and study the things we experience through our physical senses, and so we can be reassured there is a certain basis for our knowing: empirical evidence—impressions left on the human self by life's phenomena. Locke and others taught this approach to truth and knowledge, called empiricism.

During this era philosophers were also seeking a unified theory of knowledge. Each one successively tried to establish a means of knowing the truth that would be accessible to every human being. The emphasis was on objective—publicly verifiable— truth, truth that remained true despite the fluctuations of life.

Because philosophy and theology are both concerned with questions about truth,[124] Christian theology has always drunk deeply from the wells of philosophy, even in the first century, when Paul the apostle enjoined philosophical conversations with Greeks of his day (Acts 17:1–34; 1 Cor. 1:18–3:23). Indeed, both philosophy and theology have been in a two-millennia-old shared quest for truth and understanding. Philosophy primarily seeks answers through human reasoning, but much of Western philosophy has also been powerfully shaped by the Christian worldview.[125] Traditionally, theology has sought answers through mining God's revelation in history. Both philosophy and theology, especially since the Renaissance, looked for *big picture* answers. They both yearned for capital-T truth for everyone in all places and times—truth that would foster better lives. Recently that quest has been bone-jarringly criticized.

The new player on the field of Western philosophy is called postmodernism. Postmodernism holds that all truth is local. There may or may not be a reality *out there* that we can all access and interpret; postmodern scholars are not unanimous on this. They do agree though that humans interpret reality through words. Words certainly help us describe reality, but words are so powerful within each culture and in the process of human knowing that the real truth is that *we may only be processing our interpretations of reality* and not reality itself. Postmodernists are fond of saying that reality is constructed. Communities construct reality when they share, process, and shape reality together.[126] Because our interpretations and constructions are inextricably intertwined with reality itself, we may only be diagnosing ourselves instead of reality.

At this point the reader may well be thinking, "Goodness! Why so much philosophy in a book on the Holy Spirit?" Our answer concerns the work of Michael Welker. In fascinating ways Welker is a theologian who has accepted the premises of postmodern philosophy yet is not a postmodernist himself. Even so, Welker presents an understanding of God's Spirit that is nuanced and significant for its working within the general perspective, if not the central tenets themselves, of postmodernism.

Raised an Evangelical Christian in West Germany, Welker studied systematic theology at the University of Tübingen. Under Jürgen Moltmann he earned a PhD in 1973. From 1983 to 1987 Welker taught systematic theology at Tübingen, but for the past two decades he's taught at the University of Heidelberg, where he is also the chair of systematic theology. Interested in science, Welker has published extensively on the interface between theology and science.[127] Like Moltmann, his mentor, Welker has participated in ecumenical dialogue—he willingly considers multiple sources and vistas when forming theological positions.

His interest in science, particularly systems theory (an interdisciplinary theory concerning how complex systems— whether in society or nature—integrate to produce effects), has been important to his expansive interests and has shaped his theological method. Interested to investigate broad fields of knowledge, Welker's method of knowing characterizes his doctrine of the Holy Spirit: he examines particularities for glimpses of the Spirit's presence. Not assuming a universal perspective to be true or possible, Welker sifts multiple sources, gleaning truths about God's Spirit in the process.

THE HOLY SPIRIT

Welker shares with Moltmann the conviction that experience is a legitimate means of knowing, a legitimate source for discussions about God. But he represents a serious critique of Moltmann. Welker does not believe *all* life or *all* experience is a vehicle for our encountering God's Spirit. In his brilliant book *God the Spirit*,[128] Welker openly critiques Moltmann's positions and qualifies that we cannot approach God's Spirit with systematic notions of the Spirit either as life-giver, mystical force field of the universe, or a numinous entity that approaches us from somewhere else. What is Welker doing here? He is arguing against older theological-philosophical understandings that first assert what the truth is, or consists of, and then proceed to unpack subsequent understandings from that prior premise. Instead, Welker argues that the Holy Spirit approaches, and manifests himself through, particularities and specific localities. In this way God's Spirit is God's presence for each community, person, or locality and their particular characteristics.

Before we delve into the unique features of Welker's writings on God's Spirit, it will be helpful to make one more broad categorization: the important issue of method. How one proceeds to do theology may well determine the number of possible outcomes. A classic Christian method of theology is called theology *from above*. Theology from above describes God, who he is in his interior self, what he has done and what he has communicated, and then proceeds downward into life, establishing truth claims and positions. A simplistic example of theology from above: "God is love"; therefore God's actions are always loving; Christians should, it follows, always be nice; and, accordingly our greatest commitment is to establish loving policies for peaceful life together. This method works from *big picture* positions down to particulars of application. Many systematic Protestant theologians (e.g., Martin Luther, John Calvin, the Presbyterian Charles Hodge) employed a methodology of theology from above.

Another theological method is called theology *from below*. This method examines what the community of faith experiences with God, and then argues up to what truth and/or God may or must be like. Put differently, this theological method works from particulars toward held positions of organization or mutual understanding. A simplistic example of theology from below is: we experience love and illumination when we are together for the sake of Christ; therefore God must be a being who loves and illuminates. Theology from below resists generalizations and desires to learn how other people experience God and/or life. Liberation theologies and feminist theologies are those whose methodology is from below.

Neither method—theology from above or theology from below—is uniform or perfectly consistent. Theology from above is informed by an extensive history of biblical interpretation that has churned through a myriad of biblical passages, philosophical insights, and experiences—from throughout Christendom—to arrive at a shared consensus. A *big picture* position itself has been informed by many particularities interpreted from below over many centuries.

Likewise, theology from below is not a naked approach to knowledge that simply processes each and every grain of information sui generis: a unique particularity that deserves its very own understanding. The commitment to diversity that characterizes theology from below is itself informed by prior commitments from above, one of which *must be* that given particular people groups accurately understand their own particular experiences. Still, grasping these generalizations of *above* and *below* help us understand how Welker's position is unique and informative.

Welker theologizes within a broad sweep of philosophy, conversant with the kinds of philosophers who effected the rise of postmodernism. Consonant with those philosophers, Welker understands that both God and reality come at us in local and particular ways. Because of this Welker sees value in doing theology from below; for instance, his very lengthy first chapter considers local and particular experiences of God. Embracing a diversity of those experiences, Welker still maintains that we need discernment as we theologize about God's Spirit. Near his book's end he writes: "Not *every* human *experience* of *liberation and freedom* is necessarily an experience of God's Spirit."[129] Thus critiquing Moltmann, who argued that we witness God's Spirit at work whenever people are liberated from oppression, Welker also levels criticism of *big picture* theology; that is, theology from above. We must refuse systematizing God, Welker suggests, and resist universal perspectives on the Spirit.[130]

Enabling his reader to discern God's Spirit in life, Welker commits himself to a study of biblical teachings about the Spirit. Moreover, he claims, his book "could even be regarded as the first comprehensive 'biblical theology of the Holy Spirit.' "[131] Welker assumes that diverse Old Testament and New Testament passages clarify the criteria for discernment—indeed, he assumes the criteria and searches to find them in the biblical texts. In that regard, from a practical perspective, he *is* doing theology from above. Or at least from above and from below, describing his approach as *emergent*.[132] Emergent methodology is a both-and dynamic, a mutual informing of differing entities and energies, of God's Spirit working in, through, with, and for the whole creation but doing so in particular places and times for human needs and human nature.

As evident in our last five chapters, the twentieth century saw explosions of theological activity around the Holy Spirit and Trinitarian doctrine. We saw that Clark Pinnock, mostly with a theology from above, took as his assumption for all theology the being of the Trinity—God as the relations of love between Father, Son, and Spirit—and then developed specific applications of that doctrine. Such theology from above, Welker believes, should be avoided because it makes for what he considers false knowledge. Welker's preferred method is assessing assorted and varied descriptions of the Spirit's coming and actions throughout the Bible, though he rarely uses the term *Trinity* to refer to the relations of Father, Son, and Holy Spirit.[133]

From his reading of earlier portions of the Old Testament (e.g., Exodus, Judges, 1 Samuel) Welker notes that the Spirit's actions are unclear and hard to discern. The Spirit regularly works in and through individual leaders *for the sake of the community* (a constant emphasis of Welker's). Because the Spirit's pro-community work includes destruction and division, it can be difficult to discern the Spirit's role. What is clear for Welker is that God's Spirit works in situations where the community is in distress; what results is that justice, mercy, and the knowledge of God come forth from within a community.

In later Old Testament passages, particularly prophetic passages (Isaiah, Ezekiel, Joel), Welker avers that the thrust of the Spirit's actions and the prophecies again pertain to justice, mercy, and the knowledge of God. Mercy is "the sensitivity not only to the distress of other persons, but also to systematically disadvantageous arrangements and to unjust differentiation in a community, and the readiness to remove these wrongs."[134] Justice for Welker involves enacting and legislating mercy without partiality; justice involves judgments and righteousness regarding the oppressed and the weak; and justice evokes the glory of God.[135] These three—mercy, justice, and the knowledge of God—are inextricably interwoven in Welker's theology of the Spirit. Where one of these is absent, Welker argues, the Spirit of God is not at work.

In the New Testament Gospels we see the fulfillment of Old Testament passages that hoped for the promised one, the Messiah, on whom God's Spirit would rest in fullness for the sake of others. Welker asserts that Jesus' entire ministry of bringing mercy, justice, and the knowledge of God was one impelled and empowered by the Spirit. Welker correspondingly notes that blasphemy of the Holy Spirit (Matt. 12:22–32) provoked Jesus' strongest condemnation because it acutely challenged the source of his ministry. (Jesus' Jewish opponents asserted that Jesus' power was from Satan, not God.)[136] Jesus' power source was the Holy Spirit, not an unclean spirit.

With Jesus' ministry God's Spirit did many specific things in and for persons and communities: he healed people's physical maladies, drove out demons, treated women as full persons, publicly spoke with Gentiles, and preached the good news of God's salvation. Because of that specificity, Jesus is not merely a symbolic model of charity or good will; again, Welker combats universalizing theological tendencies. Jesus' diverse and particular actions performed in specific geographical locations exemplify for Welker God's desire to bless particular people around the world in diverse locations and situations.

Studying further scriptural models, Welker focuses on Pentecost (Acts 2) and its connection to the promise in Joel 2:28–29, "I will pour out my Spirit on all mankind . . . sons . . . daughters . . . old . . . young . . . male . . . and female." That verse is accordingly abbreviated because Welker's focus is not on actions—prophecies, dreams, or visions (per the verse itself)—but on the inclusive nature of the Spirit's outpouring; the community, not the works, are Welker's focus. Welker applies his communitarian interpretation of Acts 2 for today, "Those who are politically and socially subordinated, even those who do not count in a society, will experience the righteousness and glory of God and will reflect God's righteousness and glory for each other as well as for those social strata that previously alone had 'weight.' Specific dominant values and systems of order cannot limit the action of the Spirit."[137]An important implication of Welker's biblical examination is that God's Spirit can be discerned operating *outside of the community of faith*. Similar to his teacher Moltmann, Welker engages ecotheologies, liberation theologies, and feminist theologies because they promote justice, mercy, and the knowledge of God. Similar to Pannenberg, Welker insists that truth is true whether inside the Church or not. For him it follows that where we see communities—whether inside of or outside of Christianity—working for justice, mercy, and the knowledge of God, we know that God's Spirit is at work. In this way Welker argues that the Spirit of God is active on behalf of the whole creation, the whole human race, and not just those who name Christ Jesus as Lord.[138]

Welker, intrigued by particularity, moves even into creedal Christianity, to the third article of the Apostles' Creed, suggesting characterizations of the Spirit's manifestation and action. Over the centuries theologians have argued that the Spirit is the energy of God, who holds the universe together (e.g., *creator Spiritus*) and gives it life (e.g., *fons vitae*). Some of these theologians have espoused a model of God's presence called panentheism: God is present in and through his creation. Welker avoids such speculative and metaphysical models for understanding the Spirit. Instead, he insists that when the Spirit comes we see God doing the things Christians confess in the Apostles' Creed:

- Whereas the creed's third article states "the communion of saints," Welker describes this in terms of enabling people to live beyond themselves and their own self-consciousness. God's Spirit, Welker avers, heals people and creates community.

- Whereas the creed professes "the forgiveness of sins," Welker asserts this chiefly concerns breaking sin's power and producing new structural patterns in life that enable mercy, justice, and the knowledge of God. The oppressed, the weak, and the ecological environment figure prominently in Welker's thoughts about sin and forgiveness.

- Whereas the creed looks forward to "the resurrection of the body," Welker believes resurrection is something *for this life* that regards shining forth God's presence without impediment.

- Whereas the creed confesses "life everlasting," Welker interprets it such that in this fleshly life we can become temples for God's presence; we can subsequently experience a quality of life that transcends all doomed-to-fail, self-driven quests for fulfillment.[139]

Through his interpretive application of the Apostles' Creed, Welker manifests yet further his propensity to sift diverse sources for theological formulation. His emergent theology is creative and diverse and accordingly opens new vistas for theological procedure.

ABIDING INFLUENCE

Western civilization today is being jolted by seismic shockwaves respecting the human ability to know. Particularity and specificity are celebrated over grand and encompassing theorization. Welker, in his theology of God's Spirit, reflects this perspective. He emphasizes the Spirit's specific liberating actions and urges us to see God's involvement in physical, tangible life. This tendency accords with Jürgen Moltmann's this-worldly emphasis. Western Protestants are increasingly following the same trajectory: engaging their local communities, these believers maintain that Jesus of Nazareth came to effect change in the here and now—in and through physicality, fleshly existence, and the shared human structures of life—and not just offer salvation for the afterlife.

Significantly, this here-and-now emphasis involves repudiation of traditional Greek philosophy's valuing of spirit over matter. Ancient Christians, teaching about God's love for creation and seeing the incarnation as God's solidarity with physicality, similarly performed communal and societal deeds; their success was the eventual Christianization of the Roman Empire. Today, Christians are steadily reengaging society with "boots on the ground" involvement—service, mercy ministries, and social outreach—and theology like Welker's inspires them with theological grist that informs and stirs their actions. There is a renewed sense in Protestantism that believers' actions both give words integrity and are a constituent part of the good news itself based in an understanding that Jesus, in the power of the Holy Spirit, engaged his society by preaching the good news and healing people's bodies.

Further reflecting societal shifts, Welker believes theology is not just an *in-house* endeavor; theology has import for those outside Christendom. He prefers to say, like Moltmann, Pannenberg, and Pinnock, that God is not only the God of Jews or Christians; he is also the God of creation and all peoples. In this book's introduction, Paul Tillich was quoted as saying that the freedom of the Spirit is *the* Protestant principle.[140] At minimum Tillich suggested the Spirit is not bound to the Church. Pushing that emphasis, Welker sees the Christian church as just one community upon whom and through which the Spirit can work. Welker sees the Spirit as transforming creation but avoids seeing the Spirit's transformation as issuing from the work of those the Spirit of God calls together: what other theologians refer to as the body of Christ, the Church. Again, Welker prefers to use the phrase *communities* here rather than *church*. God's Spirit is free to work in various communities.

Still, God's Spirit is not present in every human experience; that would be totalizing and encompassing. With nuance, Welker urges discernment. The Spirit's presence may be discerned when mercy, justice, and the knowledge of God break forth into any community.[141] Yet experience is important for Welker's theology; this is a poignant and historic hallmark: for more than a century modernism eschewed experience for objectivity, but now the phenomenon of experience significantly matters to an influential theological titan like Welker.

Another significant shift Welker represents is a downplaying of Jesus Christ's centrality. Like Pinnock and Moltmann, Welker presents a robust Spirit-Christology. For Welker, Jesus was the bearer of the Spirit, in unprecedented ways. Spirit-Christology is something recent theologians have emphasized against older classical Logos models of Christology.

As noted repeatedly herein, Welker is celebrated for seeking new voices and insights within the Bible and other potential theological sources. An important point for him as a theologian is that he wants to allow God's Spirit to speak through diverse sources and voices. In this regard, Welker's emergent theology— allowing differing sources to shape and inform each other—is significant more for its method than any novel conclusions. Millions of Christians today likewise positively affirm the experiential realm: personal stories of God's faithfulness and testimonies of the Spirit's loving actions make profound impressions on people around the world. Indeed, the Holy Spirit seems to consistently work through people's words.

Conclusion

OB DYLAN once sang, "The times they are a changin'." Our study reveals that Protestant reflection about God's Holy Spirit is also experiencing significant development and change. The third member of the Trinity, largely neglected for centuries, is garnering reflection in unprecedented fashion. Even Pope John Paul II (r. 1978–2005) once remarked that the third millennium would likely be the era of the Holy Spirit. But this "new" development more accurately took centuries to flourish.

Protestant theological reflection about the Holy Spirit began, as did most Protestant theology, with questions about salvation: what does the Spirit do in salvation? Martin Luther's concerns about the doctrine of salvation were largely resolved by appealing to the Bible: salvation is rooted in Christ's person and work, not the Christian's person and work, and the Holy Spirit is the source of saving faith. Still, many other Protestants needed categories that personally resonated in their daily lives, and this need centered in the question of assurance: how can I know I am saved? The Anabaptists and John Wesley each answered that question in different ways, but with the shared features that the Spirit lives inside believers, conveys qualitatively new life, and yearns to transform us. We see that, with the Anabaptists and Wesley, Protestant doctrine about the Holy Spirit wrought a decidedly subjective orientation.

The subjective element in Protestant thought on the Holy Spirit was, for contextual and philosophical reasons, accentuated by Friedrich Schleiermacher. He argued that God-consciousness is central to both Christ himself and our being Christian, and that God's Spirit comes to underscore our awareness of God; experience is central to being human, and experiencing God's Spirit is central, for Schleiermacher, to being Christian. Yet Schleiermacher's subjectivizing emphasis went too far for other Protestants. Abraham Kuyper sought correction through his Reformed framework: the Spirit comes to believers in a way that makes Christ's historical and objective work subjectively alive. Karl Barth too was distressed by the shift Schleiermacher represented. Afraid that those subjectivizing tendencies turned salvation into an exclusively human enterprise, Barth highlighted God's sovereignty in salvation. Always the first mover, God, by the Holy Spirit, baptizes believers into the story and identity of Jesus with the result that Christians share in Jesus' mission, *koinōnia*, and enjoy God's indwelling presence.

In the second half of the twentieth century, the Charismatic movement's explosive influence among mainline Protestants, following the experiential trail blazed by the Pentecostal movement, turned things Holy Spirit-ual into substantive theological content and opened fresh vistas of exploration about God's Spirit. Protestant theologians like J. Rodman Williams, Jürgen Moltmann, Wolfhart Pannenberg, Clark Pinnock, and

Michael Welker explored new avenues, including the extent to which God's Spirit is present in other religions and/or the physical-temporal realm, the Spirit's role in Church mission, and how the Holy Spirit informs social justice concerns.

It is profoundly significant that the older Protestant doctrinal pattern of Word (Christ) before Spirit is increasingly being challenged. Spirit-Christology—the viewpoint that sees the Spirit as making Jesus *to be the Christ* and empowering his ministry— opens new perspectives for thinking about God's work in creation. What that means for Christianity itself is also under construction: if God, by his life-giving Spirit, works among people apart from the gospel or specific Christ-oriented categories, as some of the theologians herein espouse, precisely what is Christianity? Does God's salvation exist outside of Christian faith? These questions, particularly amid an increasingly globalized and pluralistic world, will be critical for the future self-understandings and mission of Christians everywhere.

Theology, because it looks for God's role and presence across life's myriad dimensions and issues, is exciting! The Holy Spirit—God's personal action and presence in life— comes to us where we are in life and works dynamically to transform particular people and situations. By Christ's grace, may it ever be so.

Acknowledgments

Writing this book was a joy. To this point my own theological interests have lain elsewhere: anthropology, aesthetics, postmodernism, and ecumenism. Pentecostalism emphasizes the Holy Spirit's role and place in daily life; so as a Pentecostal theologian myself, I was gratified working through the many insightful theologians reviewed herein. I am grateful to both Jon Sweeney, associate publisher, and Lil Copan, senior editor, at Paraclete Press for their valuable assistance and direction. The opportunity to contribute to Paraclete's series on God's Spirit is a privilege.

An invaluable dialogue partner during this endeavor was my colleague at Vanguard University Dr. Frank Macchia, professor of theology. His professional input and wise counsel was timely and wonderfully beneficial. Cecil M. Robeck Jr., professor of Church history and ecumenics at Fuller Theological Seminary, formerly my PhD mentor and now friend, initially contacted me about this project and also brainstormed with me on nuanced matters. Other blessings to me in the procurement of resources were Elena Nipper, Vanguard library faculty member, and William "Jack" Morgan, Vanguard librarian.

Finally, I dedicate this book to John and DyAnn Rybarczyk, my father and stepmother, who raised me in the Pentecostal tradition. Thanks, Dad and Mom, for insisting on Christian values. That heritage formed me in Christ and his dynamic presence: the holy, playful, and mysterious Spirit of God.

Glossary

Charismatics: those Christians who accept and encourage the presence and exercise of spiritual gifts (e.g., prophecy, healings, miracles, words of knowledge, speaking in tongues) but who remain in their traditional churches. Most Charismatics do not believe speaking in tongues is the only sign of the baptism of, or infilling with, the Holy Spirit. Some of the larger Christian bodies who have been deeply influenced by the Charismatic movement are Roman Catholics, Anglicans, Lutherans, Methodists, Presbyterians, and many different kinds of Baptists.

Creeds: summaries of the Christian faith (from the Greek *credo*, meaning "I believe"). Since at least the second century, Christians have summarized their essential beliefs in statements that they confess together in corporate worship services. The more famous of these are the Apostles' (second century), Nicene (325), and Chalcedonian (451) Creeds. Local creeds—that is, belief statements held by local churches or larger denominations—are usually called confessions.

Evangelicalism: This movement began early in the twentieth century in North America as a reaction to the rise of developments like German higher criticism (a movement of biblical study that often relegated the Bible to being only a document from history and lacking any eternal quality to it), Darwinian evolution (which seemed to undermine the biblical creation accounts), and proponents of the Social Gospel (that Christianity's aim was good works and transforming society, usually motivated, Evangelicals believed, by a Marxist interpretation of society). Evangelicals emphasize the following beliefs: (1) universal human sinfulness; (2) Jesus Christ as God's only means of salvation; (3) God's sovereignty; (4) the authority of the Bible for life and faith. Evangelicals emphasize the need for a conversion experience and a saving relationship with God through Jesus Christ.

Holiness movement: traces its roots back to the Pietists and emphasizes holiness in life and Christian practice. Characterizing this movement is John Wesley's doctrine of entire sanctification: one can have an experience of God that removes original sin (sometimes called the Adamic nature or the *old man*). Wesley himself also described holiness and/or sanctification in terms of love; one can be suffused with the love of God in a life-transforming manner. Holiness adherents are historically renowned for having strict lifestyle codes: no makeup or pants for women; a ban on attending dances, movies, and bowling allies; and prohibitions on alcohol and tobacco and gambling. Nearly all Holiness adherents became Pentecostals in the early twentieth century.

Humanism: a term used to connote the sixteenth-century cultural shift that sought to study people and things on their own, apart from their connections to God or beliefs about God. There was no specific philosopher who inspired or led humanism. The primary emphases of humanism were writing and speaking with eloquence and the return to Greco-Roman literary and artistic sources. The fourteenth- and fifteenth-century Renaissance was thus informed by humanism. For sixteenth-century Protestants this reference to antiquity meant returning to the Scriptures in their original languages. Humanism became a powerful vehicle of challenge to the Catholic Church tradition.

Immanence: God's presence in and through his creation as its source and sustainer. In classic Christian theology God existed before the universe, but he has not simply stepped back to let it run its course; he was not merely the divine "watchmaker" who wound it up and now lets it tick off on its own. Instead, God is the constant life-giver, the one who is ever attendant to the events and circumstances of life. For contrast, see "Transcendence" below.

Magisterial Reformers/Protestants: Groups who related to existing political structures: city councils, magistrates, and princes. Different Protestants—Lutherans, Calvinists, and Baptists—took various positions concerning church-state structures and alignments. Antonym: Radical Protestants—those who sought to sever all connections and commitments to civil authorities.

Panentheism: The belief that God is present in and through his creation, that God and creation are interrelated and shape one another. There are various positions within panentheism. Some continue to maintain God's transcendence: God is utterly free to interact with and within the universe as he pleases. Some, like process theologians, posit that God has become inseparably one with creation, so that in the universe's unfolding God is processing his own identity. An important impulse to panentheistic constructions is that God not be seen as either too distant from the world (deism) or completely one with the world (pantheism). Simplified ways to express panentheism are to say "God is the soul of the world," or, "The world is God's body."

Pentecostalism: This movement began most famously at the Azusa Street Mission in Los Angeles in 1903 under the leadership of William Seymour, a black pastor from the South. The movement emphasizes being baptized in the Holy Spirit (i.e., filled with the Spirit) and speaking in tongues. It traditionally takes the strong eschatological (end times) stance that Jesus is coming again soon. In Pentecostalism God gives his Spirit for personal transformation and empowerment for ministry. Spiritual gifts, then, are tools the Spirit gives the Church for the sake of ministry; all believers have different gifts and all are called to participate in ministry. Both Spirit baptism for empowerment and the sense of history's looming end have motivated and still motivate Pentecostal missionaries to go all over the globe sharing the gospel of Jesus Christ. Today Pentecostals are experiencing explosive growth in Africa, China, and Latin America.

Pietism: A Protestant movement that first began in seventeenth-century Europe as a reaction to formalizing Lutheranism, Pietism emphasized private Bible reading, prayer, and meeting in homes or small groups for the sake of growth in one's walk with Christ. In short, there was and is a strong emphasis on devotional Christianity in denominations and churches informed by Pietism, whose tendency is more toward practical or daily Christian living than careful theological exposition. Philip Jacob Spener (AD 1635–1705) is most commonly held to be the founder.

Salvation history: God's redemptive actions in history, and the study of this history. Traditionally this study comprises the biblical events themselves. Salvation history is thus seen as distinct from the entirety of human history, though even on this matter there are differing theological positions. Some theologians have sought to expand salvation history to include all of the redemptive and life-giving actions of God. Newer lines of argumentation run that God's actions in history have not ceased.

Transcendence: This refers to God's being above, beyond, or outside of time and space. In classic Christian theology God is the Creator of all there is, save himself. Even though he sustains the existence of the universe, he existed before time and now ultimately exists beyond the universe. For contrast, see, "Immanence" above.

Notes

INTRODUCTION

1   Paul Tillich, *The Protestant Era* (Chicago: University of Chicago Press, 1947), 94–112.

2   Georges Florovsky, *"Sobornost:* The Catholicity of the Church," in *The Church of God*, ed. E. L. Mascall (London: SPCK, 1934), 53.

3   All biblical references and quotations are from the New American Standard Bible.

1 MARTIN LUTHER

4   Regin Prenter, *Spiritus Creator: Luther's Concept of the Holy Spirit*, trans. John M. Jensen (Philadelphia: Muhlenberg Press), 1953.

5   Prenter, *Spiritus Creator*, 21.

6   Others included *sola scriptura*: Scripture alone has final authority; *sola gratia*: by grace alone. Mark Noll summarizes the Reformers' teaching as follows, "Salvation was by grace alone through faith alone as communicated with perfect authority in the Scriptures." Mark Noll, *Turning Points: Decisive Moments in the History of Christianity*, 2nd ed. (Grand Rapids: Baker Academic, 2000), 25.

7   *A Short Explanation of Dr. Martin Luther's Small Catechism, A Handbook of Christian Doctrine* (St. Louis: Concordia, 1944), 126.

8 Roman Catholicism generally held that grace was a type
   of metaphysical substance that was transmitted via the
   sacraments. God's grace was thus mediated through those
   acts and rituals, which were initiated by God himself.
   Luther countered that grace was God himself coming to
   us. Sacraments, for Luther, consisted of promises and signs.
   Promises consist in the faithfulness of God to do what he
   said he would. Signs are the instruments through which the
   promises are conveyed.

9 Prenter, *Spiritus Creator*, 104. The inner word was a witness
   or testimony to one's heart. This was a phrase used especially by Anabaptists and spiritualists of Luther's day. He
   did not deny the reality of an inner or personal word, but
   he gave primacy to the spoken and written word of God.

10 For a much more technical discussion of this element of
   Luther's theology see Prenter, *Spiritus Creator*, 110–30.

11 Ibid., 10.

12 Bloesch, *The Holy Spirit: Works and Gifts* (Downers Grove, IL:
   InterVarsity Press, 2000), 16.

13 Prenter, *Spiritus Creator*, 69.

14 *Luther's Small Catechism*, 125 (emphasis in original).

15 For a careful analysis of Luther's theology on this point see
   Bengt Hägglund, *History of Theology*, 3rd ed., trans. Gene J.
   Lund (St. Louis: Concordia, 1968), 229–31.

2 THE SIXTEENTH-CENTURY ANABAPTISTS

16 *The Complete Writings of Menno Simons*, 2nd ed., trans. and
   ed. John Christian Wenger (Scottdale, PA: Herald Press,
   1966), 90.

17 Balthasar Hubmaier, "Concerning Heretics and Those Who Burn Them (1524)," in *A Reformation Reader: Primary Texts with Introductions*, ed. Denis Janz (Minneapolis: Fortress Press, 1999), 170.

18 *The Collected Works of Thomas Müntzer*, ed. and trans. Peter Matheson (Edinburgh: T & T Clark, 1988), 380.

19 *The Complete Writings of Menno Simons*, "Triune God," 496.

20 See Kenneth Scott Latourette, *A History of Christianity*, vol. 2: *Reformation to the Present*, rev. ed. (San Francisco: HarperSanFrancisco, 1975), 778–79.

21 Contemporary global Anabaptist Mennonites now counsel against rampant individual interpretation of the Bible as an unhealthy signal. They caution against "an arbitrary and careless use of Scripture resulting from an unwillingness to submit to the discipline of serious Bible study." Later in the same document they admonish that "Christian experience, both contemporary and historical, should not be ignored in attempting to understand the Spirits [sic] work. The Scriptures, however, must remain the primary source of guidance in shaping our Christian insights and experience." Global Anabaptist Encyclopedia Online, "The Holy Spirit In the Life of the Church (Mennonite Church, 1977), A summary statement adopted by Mennonite General Assembly June 18–24, 1977, Estes Park, Colorado," www .gameo.org/encyclopedia/contents/H6583.html (accessed June 20, 2009).

22 There is no one Bible passage to account for this, but foundational passages include Matthew 16:13–19, regarding church authority, and John 6:22–65, regarding eating and

drinking Jesus. The rise of the sacramental system was a complex historical development that involved many cultural elements, not least of which was an abiding respect for wise and pious leaders.

23 *The Complete Writings of Menno Simons*, "The New Birth, c. 1537," 89.

24 Hans Denck, *Classics of the Radical Reformation*, vol. 3: *Anabaptism in Outline: Selected Primary Sources*, ed. Walter Klaassen (Scottdale, PA: Herald Press, 1981) 73.

25 Bloesch, *The Holy Spirit*, 104.

26 Denck, "Concerning True Love," in *A Reformation Reader: Primary Texts with Introductions*, ed. Denis Janz (Minneapolis: Fortress Press, 1999), 185.

27 This includes George Fox and the Quakers and individual leaders like Sebastian Franck and Caspar Schwenckfeld, in Germany, and Johannes Bünderlin, in Strasbourg and later Moravia.

3 JOHN WESLEY

28 Here I follow the analysis of Kenneth J. Collins, *The Theology of John Wesley: Holy Love and the Shape of Grace* (Nashville: Abingdon, 2007), 6–9, 20–22.

29 Albert Outler, ed., *The Works of John Wesley*, bicentennial ed. (Nashville: Abingdon, 1991), *Sermons*, 2:480–81.

30 Collins, *Theology of John Wesley*, 55.

31 Outler, *Sermons*, 2:477.

32 Collins, *Theology of John Wesley*, 4.

33 Ibid., 77–82.

34 Outler, *Sermons*, 1:287.

35 Bloesch, *The Holy Spirit*, 127.

36 Pelagius was a bishop in Britain against whom Augustine wrote some powerful treatises on salvation. The Church subsequently burned all of Pelagius's writings so that we only know of him through what the Church wrote. He is thus a kind of theological antihero in the theological systems of orthodox Christians.

4 FRIEDRICH SCHLEIERMACHER

37 Perhaps an overgeneralization, but Eastern (e.g., Slavic and Greek Orthodox) and Western (Roman Catholicism and Protestantism) Christianity can each be characterized along Platonic and Aristotelian lines, respectively.

38 Schleiermacher, *Addresses on Religion*, 1799, in Elie Kedourie, *Nationalism*, 3rd ed., Praeger University Series (London: Hutchison, 1961), 26.

39 Robert Merrihew Adams said, "The givenness of feeling does not guarantee the truth of anything we say about the feeling." Robert Merrihew Adams, "Faith and religious knowledge," in *The Cambridge Companion to Friedrich Schleiermacher*, ed. Jacqueline Mariña (Cambridge: Cambridge University Press, 2005), 39. There are numerous possible explanations for our sense of dependency, none of which presuppose God's existence. It is worthwhile to remind the reader that the historical context of his day weighed heavily on Schleiermacher.

40 That a kind of psychological analysis of Jesus from a reading of the Gospels is tenuous at best did not seem apparent to Schleiermacher. Moreover, that Schleiermacher read the

texts of the Bible with a commitment to understanding the original author's intention is both ironic and fascinating, especially as it concerns Jesus' identity. Schleiermacher was a founder of the school of authorial intent.

41 George Cross, *The Theology of Schleiermacher: A Condensed Presentation of His Chief Work, 'The Christian Faith'* (Chicago: University of Chicago Press, 1911), 325. Original source, Albert Schweitzer, *The Quest of the Historical Jesus: A Critical Study of Its Progress from Reimarus to Wrede* (Baltimore: Johns Hopkins University Press, 1998), 61.

42 To be fair, *all* theology is influenced by philosophy. The question is, what is king? What is the guiding principle or commitment?

5 ABRAHAM KUYPER

43 Kuyper argued that all people, situated as they are in their environment and time, make assumptions and faith commitments, which in turn preshape their understanding. In this way, understanding and reason are not neutral but founded on prior commitments. See Peter S. Heslam, *Creating a Christian Worldview: Abraham Kuyper's Lectures on Calvinism* (Grand Rapids: Eerdmans, 1998), 93–94.

44 Abraham Kuyper, *The Work of the Holy Spirit*, trans. Henri De Vries (1900; reprint, Grand Rapids: Eerdmans, 1973), 205.

45 John Calvin (AD 1509–64) is usually named as the founder of the Reformed tradition. Other groups within the Reformed tradition include Presbyterians, Baptists, and Congregationalists.

46 Kuyper, *Work of the Holy Spirit*, 581.

47   Ibid., 306.

48   Ibid., 73.

49   Ibid., 493, referencing Romans 7:17.

50   Ibid., 23 (emphasis in original).

51   Ibid., 39.

52   Kuyper likely knew about John Wesley's doctrine of prevenient grace, which asserted precisely the same things, but establishing any connection between the two is beyond this study's scope.

53   Kuyper, *Work of the Holy Spirit,* 417.

6 KARL BARTH

54   They commonly say things like, "Everything happens for a reason," or "God knows what he's doing even if we don't," or "Well, we prayed about it, so the election must have turned out according to God's will." Those of an Augustinian stripe are less prone to believe in luck or chance.

55   Barth argued that God's election from eternity was in Jesus. Put differently, there was no in-the-mind-of-God-for-salvation decree outside of or before Christ. Christ and his advent *was* the decree. All who would be saved would come through God's decreed one: Jesus of Nazareth. There is no salvation outside of Jesus, and on this Barth was adamant.

56   We could add that because Barth believed God and God's self-revelation were the bases of all reality, and because God is mysteriously Triune, he located the Trinity as the basis of his theological system.

57   John Thompson, *The Holy Spirit in the Theology of Karl Barth* (Eugene, OR: Pickwick, 1991), 43.

58 I am indebted to Frank Macchia for insight here. See his "Astonished by Faithfulness to God: A Reflection on Karl Barth's Understanding of Spirit Baptism," in *The Spirit and Spirituality: Essays in Honor of Russell P. Spittler*, ed. Wonsuk Ma and Robert P. Menzies (Edinburgh: T & T Clark), 164–76.

59 A Pentecostal who follows Barth on Spirit baptism as encompassing category is Frank Macchia, *Baptized in the Spirit: A Global Pentecostal Theology* (Grand Rapids: Zondervan, 2006).

60 Karl Barth, *Church Dogmatics*, IV/4, ed. G.W. Bromiley and T.F. Torrance (Edinburgh: T & T Clark, 1969), 525.

61 Thompson, *The Holy Spirit in the Theology of Karl Barth*, neatly summarizes this on 98–99.

62 Summary taken from Thompson, *The Holy Spirit in the Theology of Karl Barth*, 101.

7 J. RODMAN WILLIAMS

63 David. B. Barrett and Todd M. Johnson, "Global Statistics" in *The New International Dictionary of Pentecostal and Charismatic Movements*, rev. and expanded, ed. Stanley Burgess (Grand Rapids: Zondervan, 2002), 284–302.

64 "Rector and a Rumpus," *Newsweek*, July 4, 1960; "Speaking in Tongues," *Time*, Aug. 15, 1960.

65 J. Rodman Williams, *Renewal Theology: Systematic Theology from a Charismatic Perspective*, 3 vols. (Grand Rapids: Academie Books, 1988–91) in one volume (Zondervan Publishing, 1996).

66 Williams was clearly writing with his own constituency in mind, a conservative constituency that believed authentic

Christianity must be biblical. The three volumes of *Renewal Theology* clearly manifest an interface with biblical texts and scholarship, but whether Williams's theology is systematic or not, scholars debate. He barely engages the history of theology, the leading theologians of the day, or substantial philosophies regarding topics carefully examined and debated for centuries.

67 There are several ways one could theologically unpack this fairly universal testimony: (1) God is the God of the living; he comes to transform people where they are, and the love of God they feel is naturally extended to those around them. (2) God incarnated himself as/in Jesus of Nazareth; the active God indwells space and time in personalized ways, and believers experience this profound "in the moment" dynamic when they are in the Spirit. (3) As the Triune one, God is himself a being in relationship; to be suffused with his presence is to be relationally "lit up," so that one rather naturally loves those in proximity to oneself.

68 See Williams's still extant website: www.jrodmanwilliams .net/home2.html. Accessed July 14, 2009.

69 Williams, *Salvation, the Spirit, and Christian Living*, 13–30. The quotes are from 28 (Grand Rapids, MI: Zondervan,1990).

70 Williams, *Renewal Theology*, 38–39, 278–87.

71 Ibid., 100.

72 "Baptism in the Spirit" takes its biblical origins in John the Baptist's prophecy, "He will baptize you with the Holy Spirit and fire" (Matt. 3:11, Lk. 3:16), and in Jesus' words to the disciples, "But you shall be baptized with the Holy Spirit not many days from now" (Acts 1:5).

73 Williams, *Renewal Theology*, Ibid., 203.

74 Ibid., 200n78. He quotes from *Charles G. Finney: An Autobiography*, reprint (Old Tappan: Revell, 1966), 20–21.

75 Ibid., 211.

76 Ibid., 227n81, from Larry Tomczak, *Clap Your Hands! A Young Catholic Encounters Christ* (Plainfield, NJ: Logos International, 1973), 112–13.

8 JÜRGEN MOLTMANN

77 Jürgen Moltmann, "A Response to My Pentecostal Dialogue Partners," *Journal of Pentecostal Theology* 4 (1994), 69. He recounts this story in *The Spirit of Life: A Universal Affirmation* (Minneapolis: Fortress Press, 1992), and *The Source of Life: The Holy Spirit and the Theology of Life* (Minneapolis: Fortress Press, 1997).

78 Moltmann, *Source of Life*, 6.

79 Eschatologically oriented theology began in the nineteenth century and has many tributaries. Important developers have been Johannes Weiss, Albert Schweitzer, Wolfhart Pannenberg, and George Eldon Ladd.

80 Moltmann, *Source of Life*, 19 (emphasis in original).

81 There are Eastern Orthodox theologians who argue the very same. It's worth noting that this egalitarian understanding of God is being employed more regularly, mostly by Protestants, to argue for women's leadership in the Church. For an insightful overview of Moltmann's Trinitarian thought, see Geiko Muller-Fahrenholz, *The Kingdom and the Power: The Theology of Jürgen Moltmann* (Minneapolis: Fortress Press, 2001), 137–52.

82 Veli-Matti Kärkkäinen, *Pneumatology: The Holy Spirit in Ecumenical, International, and Contextual Perspective* (Grand Rapids: Baker Academic, 2002), 131.

83 See especially Jürgen Moltmann, *The Trinity and the Kingdom: The Doctrine of God*, trans. Margaret Kohl (San Francisco: Harper & Row, 1981), 21–60.

84 Ibid., 47. He also poignantly wrote, "The more a person believes, the more deeply he experiences pain over suffering in the world, and the more passionately he asks about God and the new creation," 49.

85 Moltmann, *Source of Life*, 119.

86 Ibid., 41.

87 Ibid., 117–20.

88 See Moltmann, *Source of Life*, 42, 62, 82, and 111–24, for themes and quotes.

89 Cf. Jürgen Moltmann, *Theology of Hope* (Minneapolis: Fortress Press, 1993); idem, *The Crucified God: The Cross of Christ as the Foundation and Criticism of Christian Theology* (Minneapolis: Fortress Press, 1993); and idem, *The Church in the Power of the Spirit* (Minneapolis: Fortress Press, 1993). Twentieth-century kingdom-of-God theology emphasizes God's sovereign—though self-limited—power; through Jesus' historic work and the Spirit's abiding presence, God's future and perfect rule breaks into the present age's kingdom of darkness and evil. Moltmann pushes against this theological stream by arguing for God's servanthood and suffering.

90 The emphasis of this point was taken from Richard Bauckham, *The Theology of Jürgen Moltmann* (Edinburgh: T & T Clark, 1995), 22.

91 Moltmann, *Spirit of Life*, 5, 17.

92 Moltmann, *Source of Life*, 62.

93 Ibid., 55. See also 68, 94, 116.

94 Ibid., 88.

95 Michael Welker, *God the Spirit*, trans. John F. Hoffmeyer (Minneapolis: Fortress Press, 1994), 19n36. We will examine Welker later in this study.

9 WOLFHART PANNENBERG

96 Wolfhart Pannenberg, "God's Presence in History," *Christian Century* 98, no. 3 (1981): 261.

97 John Dillenberger and Claude Welch, *Protestant Christianity: Interpreted Through Its Development*, 2nd ed. (New York: Macmillan, 1988), 313.

98 Universalism: the belief that all people in all places and times will eventually come to salvation, despite their various and competing beliefs, values, or morals.

99 This overview of Pannenberg's commitments is drawn from Stanley Grenz, *Reason for Hope: The Systematic Theology of Wolfhart Pannenberg*, 2nd ed. (Grand Rapids: Eerdmans, 2005), 6–10.

100 See ibid., 143–45, 293.

101 F. LeRon Shults, "Spirit and Spirituality: Philosophical Trends in Late Modern Pneumatology," *Pneuma: The Journal of the Society for Pentecostal Studies* 30 (2008): 280–81.

102 Veli-Matti Kärkkäinen, *Pneumatology: The Holy Spirit in Ecumenical, International, and Contextual Perspective* (Grand Rapids: Baker Academic, 2002), 122.

103 General revelation is that which can be known about God through studying his creation. Special revelation is that which God alone reveals. General revelation is not held to be salvific, but special revelation is. Pannenberg doesn't make this distinction because of his commitment to the universal quality of all truth and that all truth points to God.

104 See Grenz, *Reason for Hope*, 49–55.

10 CLARK PINNOCK

105 Conservatives in the many churches (Roman Catholicism, Eastern Orthodoxy, and the many Protestantisms) are often wary of ecumenism. They see it as a vehicle that provokes compromise. We must add, though, that laypeople tend to be less resistant to diversity than church leaders. The latter have more at stake than the former.

106 For example, the reader may be surprised to know that the International Roman Catholic-Pentecostal dialogue has been at work since 1972 and completed its fifth session in 2007. This dialogue has support from the Pontifical Council for Promoting Christian Unity.

107 Emergent churches are Protestant churches that seek to get beyond denominationalism, something they view as a hindrance. Their focus is local, not global, and their ethos is postmodern rather than modern. They are characterized by an interest in liturgical and aesthetic experimentation, experience rather than doctrine, and consistently target a specific socioeconomic demographic.

108 See my own, *Beyond Salvation: Eastern Orthodoxy and Classical Pentecostalism on Becoming Like Christ* (Milton Keynes: Paternoster, 2004).

109 Kilian McDonnell and George T. Montague, *Christian Initiation and Baptism in the Holy Spirit: Evidence from the First Eight Centuries* (Collegeville, MN: Liturgical, 1991, 1994).

110 Most notably on this point is *Evangelicals and Catholics Together: The Christian Mission in the Third Millennium.* Their first document was published in 1994. Those involved have produced subsequent reports on salvation, Scripture and tradition, and the communion of the saints. Led by the Roman Catholics Richard John Neuhaus and Cardinal Avery Dulles (deceased within a month of each other, in late 2008 and early 2009) and the Protestant Charles Colson, this dialogue and the reports it has produced have been both warmly embraced and caustically criticized by differing folks on all sides.

111 For example, Clark Pinnock, *A Defense of Biblical Infallibility* (Philadelphia: Presbyterian & Reformed, 1967); idem, *Reason Enough: A Case for the Christian Faith* (Downers Grove, IL: InterVarsity Press, 1980).

112 Clark Pinnock, *The Openness of God* (Downers Grove, IL: InterVarsity Press, 1994). Theology of the openness of God says that God, instead of micromanaging every single event and instance in life, is open toward life and creation. It is an attempt to take more seriously the biblical witness, which portrays angels, human beings, and even nations as having free will and power to sustain or thwart God's will. Particularly, open theology says God is open to the future:

God moves dynamically in and through creation and free willing, accomplishing his purposes. Some open theologians say that God does not exhaustively know the future because the future is by definition unknowable, by anyone.

113 There are various annihilationist positions. Pinnock believed that hell is real but not eternal. Those judged to hell will eventually cease to exist. See his own chapter and his responses to others in William Crockett, Zachary Hayes, Clark Pinnock, and John Walvoord, *Four Views on Hell* (Grand Rapids: Zondervan, 1996).

114 Clark Pinnock, *A Wideness in God's Mercy: The Finality of Jesus Christ in a World of Religions* (Grand Rapids: Zondervan, 1992).

115 Clark Pinnock, *Flame of Love: A Theology of The Holy Spirit* (Downers Grove, IL: InterVarsity Press, 1996).

116 It is curious that Pinnock did this, because the Eastern Orthodox for centuries have argued that the Augustinian model depersonalizes the Spirit. Pinnock either overlooked this or was not troubled by it.

117 Pinnock, *Flame of Love*, 21 (emphasis added).

118 Ibid., 50.

119 Ibid., 51.

120 Ibid., 64.

121 The Church has historically subordinated God's Spirit to Christ, though arguably for sound reasons. The biblical narrative clearly portrays that Jesus sent the Holy Spirit to his Church (Jn. 14, 16; Acts 1–2). The Epistles either refer to the Spirit as the Spirit of Christ (Rom. 8:2, 9) or qualify the Holy Spirit's work in relation to the work of

Christ Jesus (as seen in our chapter on Luther). Traditional understandings of salvation and redemption are rooted in Christ, and the Spirit's descent is understood as an element of Christ's redemptive work. Church doctrine (ecclesiology) has consistently understood that grace is rooted in the person and work of Jesus—the Spirit comes to make real what Christ has accomplished; we saw this earlier in this study: the Spirit comes to make subjectively real what Christ objectively accomplished in history. Sacramental Christians (Roman Catholics, Eastern Orthodox, Anglicans, and others) believe God's grace is obtained for us through Christ's incarnation, atonement, and resurrection and that the Spirit comes to transmit that grace through the sacraments. So there are many important reasons in Church history why the Spirit was subordinated to Jesus, even if that affects Trinitarian formation.

122 Pinnock, *Flame of Love*, 82. Pinnock was not at all the first to espouse what is known as Spirit-Christology. Schleiermacher had presented Jesus in similar, though philosophized, form nearly 170 years earlier. More recently Geoffrey Lampe, *God as Spirit* (Minneapolis: Fortress Press, 1984), has presented Jesus as a man used of the Spirit. Pinnock is rather unique, however, in being an evangelical who embraces Spirit-Christology.

123 Pinnock, *Flame of Love*, 188.

11 MICHAEL WELKER

124 Pope Benedict XVI shares brilliant reflections on the interaction between philosophy and Christian theology in

his book *Truth and Tolerance: Christian Belief and World Religions*, trans. Henry Taylor (San Francisco: Ignatius, 2004), 138–97.

125 For instance, the following beliefs have been decisive guidelines for Western philosophy and science: (1) there is a God who created the universe; (2) the universe was created in an orderly way such that human beings can understand it; (3) God is a good God, whose moral commandments and revelations are beneficial for the human race. Cf. Kenneth S. Latourette, *A History of Christianity, Beginnings to 1500*, rev. ed. (New York: Harper & Row, 1975), 605.

126 In my own classes I describe this as "group relativism." It is not a matter of some creative or gifted individual thinker coming up with answers. It is not a matter of each person having his or her own opinion. It is a matter of how entire linguistic groupings and clusters of people process reality and arrive at truth. The collective dimensions are critical for an accurate understanding of postmodernism. We can see then why multiculturalism has become a powerful player in Western society: each culture is unique and to be respected for its own appropriation of reality.

127 Michael Welker, *Creation and Reality* (Minneapolis: Fortress Press, 1999); idem, *The End of the World and the Ends of God: Science and Theology on Eschatology* (Harrisburg: Trinity Press International, 2000); idem, ed., *Resurrection: Theological and Scientific Assessments* (Grand Rapids: Eerdmans, 2002).

128 Michael Welker, *God the Spirit*, trans. John F. Hoffmeyer (Minneapolis: Fortress Press, 1994).

129 Ibid., 336 (emphasis in original).

130 Ibid., x, 25, 26, 41, 47, 161–62, 223.

131 Ibid., xii.

132 Ibid., 28, 99, 251. He ascribes his indebtedness to Alfred North Whitehead (1861–1947) on emergent philosophy.

133 Ibid., xi, 240n25.

134 Ibid., 119.

135 Ibid., 108–18.

136 Ibid., 339.

137 Ibid., 127–28.

138 Welker also argues for the public/inclusive thrust of the Spirit's work in that Balaam, a non-Israelite, shared in God's perspective on reality, ibid. 97–98, and that the Spirit as wind in the Old Testament makes evident that God's actions are not isolated to the nation of Israel, 100.

139 Ibid., 65, 283–341.

140 Paul Tillich, *The Protestant Era* (Chicago: University of Chicago Press, 1947), 94–112.

141 Some scholars wonder if Welker's repeated triad—mercy, justice, and the knowledge of God—work as a dogmatic grid or an established form of interpretive truth, something against which he repeatedly rails in his work. Others see Welker's interpretive bias particularly evident in his many critiques of Western society for its abuses and injustices. He is angry with the West for its ecological pollution, market economies, media manipulation, and amassing of nuclear weaponry. With Welker, the rest of the world's many atrocities receive a pass.

ABOUT PARACLETE PRESS
WHO WE ARE

Paraclete Press is a publisher of books, recordings, and DVDs on Christian spirituality. Our publishing represents a full expression of Christian belief and practice—from Catholic to Evangelical, from Protestant to Orthodox.

We are the publishing arm of the Community of Jesus, an ecumenical monastic community in the Benedictine tradition. As such, we are uniquely positioned in the marketplace without connection to a large corporation and with informal relationships to many branches and denominations of faith.

WHAT WE ARE DOING

BOOKS. Paraclete publishes books that show the richness and depth of what it means to be Christian. Although Benedictine spirituality is at the heart of all that we do, we publish books that reflect the Christian experience across many cultures, time periods, and houses of worship. We publish books that nourish the vibrant life of the church and its people—books about spiritual practice, formation, history, ideas, and customs.

We have several different series, including the best-selling Paraclete Essentials, and Paraclete Giants series of classic texts in contemporary English; A Voice from the Monastery—men and women monastics writing about living a spiritual life today; award-winning literary faith fiction and poetry; and the Active Prayer Series that brings creativity and liveliness to any life of prayer.

RECORDINGS. From Gregorian chant to contemporary American choral works, our music recordings celebrate sacred choral music through the centuries. Paraclete distributes the recordings of the internationally acclaimed choir Gloriæ Dei Cantores, praised for their "rapt and fathomless spiritual intensity" by *American Record Guide*, and the Gloriæ Dei Cantores Schola, which specializes in the study and performance of Gregorian chant. Paraclete is also the exclusive North American distributor of the recordings of the Monastic Choir of St. Peter's Abbey in Solesmes, France, long considered to be a leading authority on Gregorian chant.

DVDS. Our DVDs offer spiritual help, healing, and biblical guidance for life issues: grief and loss, marriage, forgiveness, anger management, facing death, and spiritual formation.

LEARN MORE ABOUT US AT OUR WEBSITE:
www.paracletepress.com, or call us toll-free at 1-800-451-5006.

ALSO IN THIS SERIES . . .

GIVER OF LIFE
THE HOLY SPIRIT IN ORTHODOX TRADITION
BY FR. JOHN W. OLIVER

*D*elving deep and subtly into Orthodox tradition and theology, *Giver of Life* articulates the identity of the Holy Spirit as the third Person of the Trinity as well as the role of the Holy Spirit in the salvation of the world. Written with a poetic sensibility, Fr. Oliver begins with Pentecost, an event uniquely celebrated in Orthodoxy as a time when greenery of all kinds is brought into churches.

Reflecting on the relationship of the Holy Spirit to the Church, to the world, and to the human person, *Giver of Life* looks to the impressive biblical and liturgical tradition of Orthodox Christianity. This is a book weighty in content but accessible in tone, not an academic study of the mind, but a lived experience of the heart.

$15.99 • TRADE PAPERBACK • ISBN: 978-1-55725-675-1

AVAILABLE FROM MOST BOOKSELLERS OR THROUGH PARACLETE PRESS
WWW.PARACLETEPRESS.COM; 1-800-451-5006.